I am an African

the
Brotherhood of Man

Cedric de la Harpe

April 06, 2018

I am an African

the
Brotherhood of Man

Cedric de la Harpe

April 06, 2018

Cedric Kaalvoet de la Harpe

As much of the research and information gathered in this manuscript, originate through the 'spiritual energy', any likeness to any living person is unintentional, all persons and places are fictitious, our respected leaders who have passed on, the information gathered, may not represent their accepted principles as recorded.

My barefoot, a symbol of taking white feet into the Townships, where we will find the answers to our integration problems.

safari@tasteofafrica.co.za   +27 82 565 2520
Revised: April 30, 2018

index

thanks to my wife and all our 'families'

<u>I am 'THE' Most Superior White</u>

About the author, by the author

What have I done to the African,
the origins of the human race,
when I arrived in Africa,
the African was nothing,
we built South Africa,
we built the African.

I was welcomed by the people,
embodied in humanity,
I arrived with the triad,
Liberty, Equality, Fraternity,
it did not take me long,
to remove Liberty and Equality.

I coerced the African to fight my wars,
never an objection received,
the Africans were the victors,
as my war ends, the Africans are united,
their graduation was self-determination,
but as the Coloniser, I failed.

I remoulded many an African,
as civilised as me,
I have freed many of them,
from their cultural practices,
they are now acceptable,
around my boardroom table.

They are my trusted indunas,
they are my wealth protector,
they continue to subjugate,
and to control the uncivilised,
they do not allow the words,
white capitalist monopoly.

I have never understood,
how all Africans could love me,
as I move through their world,
embodied in humanity,
their African energy
ignites the fire in me.

I see people of all colours
scattered around me,
I see you can be Black,
but not be an African,

*you can be Black,
with an 'European' culture.*

*I understand that as a white,
you can be African,
not because,
you were born in Africa,
just embody yourself,
in the humanity of Africa.*

*Today I feel so proud,
Africa has blessed me,
with direct access to,
its world of humanity,
a world of no hate,
for other human-beings,*

*Where no individual,
benefits at the expense of an African,
a world where colour does not define,
where humanity embodies us all,
Today I am THE Most Superior White,
I am an African.*

Cedric Kaalvoet de la Harpe

<u>*I am an African*</u>

Since 2013, I have not stopped researching South Africa's history, I started because our Government was spending millions on commemorating the 1913 Native Land Act, and I needed to find out who we were before 1913, and how we got from 1913, to today.

For three months, I 'Google research', and find nothing new, the Frontier Wars, the Zulu Wars, the Mfecane, the two ZARepublics, the Anglo Boer War, finding no signs that we, the Coloniser, had not complied with 'Internationally accepted Standards'.

Then one night, or rather 02:00 in the morning, 'Baboon' one of my visiting spirits, orangish in colour, almost orangutang features, stands over my bed, and his voice is very clear, strangely calm for his large frame;
> *"Cedric, continue doing what you are doing, but start looking at what you see, through the eyes of an African leader."*

I jumped out of bed, and started to study the files on my computer, and it did not take long, for me to see our lives differently, within six weeks, I am of the opinion that;

"If it was not for what we, the English Coloniser did, our African population would be the wealth of South Africa today, Townships would not exist, and African poverty would not exist."

I have not stopped researching and writing, using extracts found on the web, not necessarily giving credit to the author, as my mindset reads the content differently to the author, my 2014 to 2105 mindset, interpreted content through 'black eyes', and from 2017, I start to see the same content differently, I now see them through an 'African eye'.

You will appreciate that I now lay claim to the status of, 'I am now an African', and I make no apologies, I also make no effort to try and motivate my claim, other than the following comment;

For some 14 years, I have integrated into the Township and Rural Village communities, often referred to by locals as the 'White Zulu', or, the 'black in a white skin'.

I however, knew myself well enough, never to refer to myself as an African, none of the "I am African, because I was born here."

I attended the WWPAC 2016 convention in Orlando East, Soweto, June 14, 2016 I was accepted during the registration process, paid my fee, R750.00, and enjoyed the conversation around our table, as we waited for the day's proceedings to start.

Then, as the proceedings started, Bheki Gumbi was invited out of the meeting, I anticipated what was coming. Five minutes later, I was invited out of the meeting. Had my registration not taken place, I would not have felt as bad, but as one of the organisers asked me to leave, I hurt, when I was told that I had no concern about Africa, about Black people, and that I had a superior white attitude?

Evicted because I was white.

That afternoon, sitting at home, I asked myself, whether we have wasted the past ten years of our lives, in an attempt to make a change.

I asked myself, how do my white minority rights protect me, this is one contravention of our Constitution, and how can a white complain to the authorities?

Today, I apologise to the WWPAC leaders who evicted me, I still believe that they were wrong, but I was not African enough to defend my eviction, I did my 'white thing', I relied on my Constitutional rights, rights I no longer respect, had I understood an African, I would have used the African humanity behaviour, to ensure that I was accepted.

What changes have taken place in my mindset, that has changed my life, and that requires me to revise the manner in which I have, until today, described our people and the countries situation?

Today, I see the world through different eyes, a few months back, I would have described my mindset, as looking at the world through a 'black leaders' eye, confirming my white superior attitude, and looking at life from a different eye, but still a white eye.

I can't identify the exact period when I started to look through a different mindset, when the landscape that I was looking at changed, when I saw the people walking the streets differently, when the streets started to look different.

Suddenly I was no longer seeing White and Black people, today I see the European White Capitalist Monopoly group, in the suburbs, the "Non-African", and on the other side, I see the African that I have subjugated, that African that I did not consider civilised, I see and feel the African.

The African in mainly Black, all shades of dark, some light, almost white.

As I look towards the Government Corruption, the Private sectors economic policy, the White Capitalist Monopoly, where executive incomes and bonuses are excessive, where the white property rights and the economy, is considered, before the African's needs and circumstances, my African mindset sees that our Country has many Black people, with African heritage, who have abandoned their cultivated defined humanity lifestyle, having allowed their Capitalist colleagues, to convince them that the Capitalist economy, allows them as an individual, within our New Democracy and Constitution, to achieve abnormal maximum income and wealth, at the expense of the African majority, still subjugated by the Capitalist, I see Black people, no longer African, as defined by the African 'humanity', I see black people, who are Non-African.

***

This manuscript initially was titled 'Brotherhood of Man' and during the process, the task of writing changes my life, for the first time I understand the African, the people that I subjugated for hundreds of years, and yet, no matter where I move through the country, the African shows only love and respect to me, his oppressor. I chose the title 'Brotherhood of Man', as I wished to avoid the many academic theories that abound around the "Ubuntu" concept.

"Ubuntu" has become a 'political philosophy', in an attempt to convince communities going through self-determination transition, that we are 'all' humane, and that we all wish to share, and I have heard many white South Africans, loudly claim 'we all participate in Ubuntu, it is South Africa', I challenge those Non-Africans, who believe they live a life embodied by Ubuntu, to make contact with the writer, who offers a free full assessment.

Fourteen years of integration into the African culture and communities, participating in the Ubuntu of the African, before I understand that I am African, because I share myself, I respect the African for their life, embodied in humanity to all.

'Humane' and 'Humanity' words used often to describe Ubuntu, but the exact definitions, could mean any number of concepts.

Ubuntu, as found in African Culture, has great similarities with 'humanity' that exists in the very conservative Afrikaner / Boer culture, during my life, I have interacted extensively with the Afrikaans community, and what I today understand as Ubuntu in my African position, has a great similarity in my

Afrikaner family community, but with one difference, it does not extend beyond the boundaries of their group.

My African persona, puts it down to religion, and prefer not to comment on the Afrikaner religion, save to say that it has divided the Afrikaner grouping, as effectively as the 'love / hate the white' divides the PAC.

Thanks to input from Credo Mutwa, my observation with regard to the humanity that defines the African, is based on their African religion, where, God and man are never seen as separate from one-another, that God exists in nature, the trees, plants, animals, that all of life together with God, forms a unified whole in which everything is interconnected, interrelated, and interdependent, *and all life is considered to be Sacred.*

I believe that the young African, whether aware of the old religious beliefs or not, has been cultivated within the above defined humanity, and as such, they live their lives embodied by this lifestyle structure, unable to operate outside of this lifestyle, unable not to love and respect other humans.

My call to fellow Africans, is that a mind that is cultivated to see different groups negatively, in my case, a racist mindset, my mind is unable to see the black person differently to how I was cultivated, thanks to great support from the African, I have achieved the status of 'racist in recovery', a cultivated mindset can never change, it can never heal, like the alcoholic, I need to stay close to my 'sponsors', attend the African forums, in order to ensure that I never fall off the wagon.

The African's ability to live their lives, embodied within their humane lifestyle, carries with them, the healing power to assist the racist white superior community member, to achieve the status of racist in recovery, and African.

As an African, guided by the humanity lifestyle, believing in the humanity lifestyle, I have numerous challenges, and trust that, by the last chapter of the manuscript, I am able to contribute towards the following social and criminal issues, that are disturbing our country:

1:   Why is crime so high, and why does life have such little value, that you can be shot for a cell-phone?

2:   Why are the white farmers being murdered, and the ANC Government does not react?

3:   Why are politicians allowed to use 'One Settler, One Bullet'?

4:   Why do we have so much domestic violence?

Cedric Kaalvoet de la Harpe, "I am an African".

Globalization Fear

I introduce you to South Africa's two political protagonists of the black struggle history, who both played for the same soccer team in December 1949. It was only a few years later, when things on the soccer field became tense, that one of them took to the boxing ring, to bring power to his political fight.

This protagonist, President Nelson Mandela, is worshipped by every white person in the World, including South African whites, for bringing freedom to our blacks, although, the white celebration indicates, that they may have benefitted more than the still subjugated African.

As a white South African, I am not afraid to admit that I was never anti-Apartheid, did not celebrate the fall of the white Government, and never developed the hero-worship, that my white brothers have developed for Mandela. This indifference to Mandela, has allowed me to read between the lines, and today, I consider Mandela to have 'sold out' the Africanist in Africa, as many of our youth today, consider him a sell-out.

Sell-Out a betrayal of one's principles for reasons of expedience.

Every African child, who has their personal origins in the Townships or Rural Villages, when going through puberty, initiation into manhood, initiation into womanhood, graduates with an Africanist mindset, when they think African before they think white.

Sidebar:

Here I need to define what I mean by the 'Africanist mindset', very simply, the mindset that dictates that the their thought process is "think African, before you think White", as I move forward, I endeavour to separate the black and white issues in our country, to one of African and Non-African, bringing a new dimension to the solutions that are possible.

This mindset resides in all of us, we all protect our heritage, our property, our families, and when threatened, many of us behave rashly, and we need to be tolerant as we move forward.

I wish that the anti-racism control measures that we have introduced in our country, were allocated to a Tribal Authority to resolve, a person, accused of being racist, should sit under the large tree, where the Commissioner and twenty elders, sitting around in a large circle, ask questions, they have a choice, as to whether they ask the accuser, or the accused, who answers the question.

The hearing moves around the circle, every elder getting an opportunity to ask their question, and when complete, the Commissioners will deliberate, and make a decision.

Every decision made, is in the interests firstly of the community, and secondly, to repair the damage done, and restore an amicable relationship between the accuser and the accused.

May I add that I was cultivated as a racist, I still am racist, but I am a racist in recovery, like an alcoholic, your mind never heals, and I need to attend the AA forum regularly, to avoid falling off the wagon?

We continue:

The Africanist will accuse the white as having considered the African in the diminutive, a Robert Sobukwe quote;

It is this group which conceives of the African people as a child nation, composed of Boys and Girls, ranging in age from 120 years to one day.

As far back as I can remember, and I was born in 1947, I never saw the black people as a nation, or a majority population, not only did we address the African as 'you', but always in the diminutive, but no matter how violent the protest was, we never believed that the majority of the African group, felt any anger, it was always the small minority group.

We would immediately attribute it towards the 'small minority' the small radical group, and this is how the media identified the 2015 'Fees Must Fall' participants that were involved in the violent destruction.

I have interacted with student leaders, who, delegated by the ANC or the DA, in theory they were not Africanist, but when the violence and burnings take place, their Africanist spirit was bubbling.

Today, as we move towards the 2019 general election, we find the 'Africanist' mindset that is bubbling in the youth, very evident in both the ANC and DA mindsets, as the struggle for control of the 'pound' takes place, we are watching a repeat of the French Revolution, where the poverty rises up against the 'Monarchy', while the Globalization Participants, sit back and manipulate the outcome, all in the interests of protecting their ill-gotten gains.

When these protests take place, by us attributing the problems to the small radical minority, we give the world the impression that the problem does not exist, and strangely, it gives us comfort. However, the Globalization participants, those who carry the money bags, have seen this behaviour often over the past 400 years, and every incident, no matter what the media says, it triggers a reaction within the Globalization participants, as they manipulate the reaction by the politicians, to protect their ill-gotten gains.

Our second protagonist, is Mangaliso Robert Sobukwe, white South Africans, or some of us, would remember him as the Pan Africanist leader, who 'allegedly' influenced the anti-white attitude towards us.

At the December 1949 ANC annual conference, the ANCYL[1], of which both protagonists were leaders, proposed the 1949 Programme of Action, including the Bill of Rights[2], which was ratified by the ANC national executive, confirming the unity of the African in Southern Africa, a unity based on the concept of Africanist Nationalism, one nation, no longer the tribal separations that the Coloniser implemented between 1835 and 1936.

Our two protagonists had the same political philosophy and principles in 1949, Africanist Nationalism, the uniting of the African with one common cause, freedom from subjugation, aimed at achieving the western maxim, "Liberty. Equality, Fraternity", loudly claimed by the European, but never achieved by the whites.

This Africanist Nationalism, is the enemy of Globalization, the White Capitalist Monopoly, most

---

[1] *Africanist Nationalist Congress Youth League*

[2] *Bill of Rights, pdf copy available electronically from the author on request*

Africanists will challenge this concept, why? Globalization, has brought them fancy cell phones, communication, fancy clothing brands, motor cars, and our favourite food, stay with me, and let me explain.

All of us know the protagonist Nelson Mandela's story, the 'Long Walk to Freedom', it has become what Kaalvoet calls 'our bible' that we are supposed to live by, it is 'our history' as defined by the Globalization participants.

As a country, that respects all religions, to the extent that it is removed from the school curriculum, when the media, the politicians, the business people, the activists, wish to guide us back onto the 'straight and narrow', Nelson Mandela's 'verses' from the Long Walk to Freedom, is always quoted.

We let Nelson Mandela, the 1949 African Nationalist, in his auto-biography, the Long Walk to Freedom, guide us through what was happening in South Africa between 1940 and 1949.

Long Walk to Freedom

Change was in the air in the 1940s. The Atlantic Charter of 1941, signed by Roosevelt and Churchill, reaffirmed faith in the dignity of each human being and propagated a host of democratic principles. Some in the West saw the charter as empty promises, but not those of us in Africa. Inspired by the Atlantic Charter and the fight of the Allies against tyranny and oppression, the ANC created its own charter, called African Claims, which called for full citizenship for all Africans, the right to buy land, and the repeal of all discriminatory legislation. We hoped that the government and ordinary South Africans would see that the principles they were fighting for in Europe were the same ones we were advocating at home.

The South African Africanist, unite off the Atlantic Charter, we will not belabour this manuscript for full details, other than the third point of the charter, the one that Churchill and his Government feared, the motivation for decolonisation, this English fear, was as the result of the USA fear of the Black, turning to Russia, for their support to obtain self-determination,

THIRD POINT
- THE RIGHT TO CHOOSE THE FORM OF GOVERNMENT..

"They respect the right of all peoples to choose the form of government under which they will live; and they wish to see sovereign rights and self government restored to those who have been forcibly deprived of them."

Kaalvoet Comment:

Europe became trapped between the two major powers, the USA, and the USSR, the Atlantic Charter was driven by the USA, believing that as the Africanist wished for self-determination, it should be given it to them, before the Russians, take the mineral 'pie'. As the years pass, the media will give the Nationalist Party, the credit, or the blame, for the political slogans, of 'Rooi Gevaar'[3], and 'Swart Gevaar'[4], but it was the USA, and these slogans gave birth, to the Atlantic Charter, and would eventually become one of the many slogans, filtered into our lives, and credited to the NP, as they were manipulated into political power.

The Africans in Southern Africa, the ANC and all other interest groups, united, prepare their 'African Claims' charter document, and includes a 'Bill of Rights', and we recall the covering letter.

The Covering letter from A B Xuma, Atlantic Charter.

As African leaders we are not so foolish as to believe that because we have made these declarations that our government will grant us our claims for the

---

[3] *Communist threat*

[4] *Black danger, black fear*

mere asking. We realise that for the African this is only a beginning of a long struggle entailing great sacrifices of them, means and even life itself.

To the African people the declaration is a challenge to organise and unite themselves under the mass liberation movement, the African National Congress. The struggle is on right now and it must be persistent and insistent. In a mass liberation movement there is no room for divisions or for personal ambitions. The goal is one, namely, freedom for all. It should be the central and only aim for objective of all true African nationals. Divisions and gratificational of personal ambitions under the circumstances will be a betrayal of this great cause.

On behalf of my Committee and the African National Congress I call upon chiefs, ministers of religion, teachers, professional men, men and women of all ranks and classes to organise our people, to close ranks and take their place in this mass liberation movement and struggle, expressed in this Bill of Citizenship Rights until freedom, right and justice are won for all races and colours to the honour and glory of the Union of South Africa whose ideals - freedom, democracy, Christianity and human decency cannot be attained until all races in South Africa participate in them.

I am confident that all men and women of goodwill of all races and nations will see the justice of our cause and stand with us and support us in our struggle.

If you ever feel discouraged in the struggle that must follow remember the wise and encouraging words of the Prime Minister, Field Marshal the Right Honourable J.C. Smuts who says: "Do not mind being called agitators. Let them call you any names they like, but get on with the job and see that matters that vitally require attention, Native health, Native food, the treatment of Native children and all those cognate questions that are basic to the welfare of South Africa are attended to."
A.B. XUMA

The African Claims charter, and a "Bill of Rights" was ratified by the ANC at their December 1943 annual conference, and was presented to Prime Minister, Jan Smuts, who rejected it.

Long Walk to Freedom

One night in 1943 I met Anton Lembede, who held master of arts and bachelor of law degrees, and A. P. Mda. From the moment I heard Lembede speak, I knew I was seeing a magnetic personality who thought in original and often startling ways. He was then one of a handful of African lawyers in all of South Africa and was the legal partner of the venerable Dr. Pixley ka Seme, one of the founders of the ANC.

Lembede said that Africa was a black man's continent, and it was up to Africans to reassert themselves and reclaim what was rightfully theirs. He hated the idea of the black inferiority complex and castigated what he called the worship and idolization of the West and their ideas. The inferiority complex, he affirmed, was the greatest barrier to liberation. He noted that wherever the African had been given the opportunity, he was capable of developing to the same extent as the white man, citing such African heroes as Marcus Garvey, W. E. B. Du Bois, and Haile Selassie. "The color of my skin is beautiful," he said, "like the black soil of Mother Africa." He believed blacks had to improve their own self-image before they could initiate successful mass action.

He preached self-reliance and self-determination, and called his philosophy Africanism. We took it for granted that one day he would lead the ANC.

Lembede declared that a new spirit was stirring among the people, that ethnic differences were melting away, that young men and women thought of themselves as Africans first and foremost, not as Xhosas or Ndebeles or Tswanas.

Lembede, whose father was an illiterate Zulu peasant from Natal, had trained as a teacher at Adam's

College, an American Board of Missions institution. He had taught for years in the Orange Free State, learned Afrikaans, and came to see Afrikaner nationalism as a prototype of African nationalism.

As Lembede later wrote in the newspaper Inkundla ya Bantu, an African newspaper in Natal:

The history of modern times is the history of nationalism. Nationalism has been tested in the people's struggles and the fires of battle and found to be the only antidote against foreign rule and modern imperialism. It is for that reason that the great imperialistic powers feverishly endeavor with all their might to discourage and eradicate all nationalistic tendencies among their alien subjects; for that purpose huge and enormous sums of money are lavishly expended on propaganda against nationalism which is dismissed as "narrow," "barbarous," "uncultured," "devilish," etc. Some alien subjects become dupes of this sinister propaganda and consequently become tools or instruments of imperialism for which great service they are highly praised by the imperialistic power and showered with such epithets as "cultured," "liberal," "progressive," "broadminded," etc.

Lembede's views struck a chord in me. I, too, had been susceptible to paternalistic British colonialism and the appeal of being perceived by whites as "cultured" and "progressive" and "civilized." I was already on my way to being drawn into the black elite that Britain sought to create in Africa.

That is what everyone from the regent to Mr. Sidelsky had wanted for me. But it was an illusion. **Like Lembede, I came to see the antidote as militant African nationalism.** *Lembede's friend and partner was Peter Mda, better known as A.P. While Lembede tended to imprecision and was inclined to be verbose, Mda was controlled and exact. Lembede could be vague and mystical; Mda was specific and scientific. Mda's practicality was a perfect foil for Lembede's idealism.*

Kaalvoet would like to interject, and make a comment that Lembede had moved Nelson Mandela, into the Africanist Nationalist mindset, and the danger that we are all faced with, is that, should you loose your 'sponsor' you will fall off the wagon. I am a racist in recovery, I need to attend regular forums to keep me in recovery, if I separate from my forum and sponsors, I will fall off the wagon.

Anton Lembede dies in 1947, and it does not take long for Nelson Mandela to return to the black elite that Britain sought to create in Africa.

From 1940, the gold mining industry's South African labour contingent from Umtata, reduced drastically, the industry balancing the losses with labour from Mozambique and Lesotho.

Was it the reluctance of the Thembu and Mfengu, to work on the mines, or, was the Africanist philosophy, the Africanist Nationalist, disturbing the employer wish to employ the South African?

<u>Decolonization after WWII</u>

As South Africans, looking at our History, and the Kaalvoet theory on the political manipulations, the Coloniser, the English and the French, were already facing decolonization conflict;

<u>French:</u>

France also had to cope with demands for independence from its colonies. On 2 September 1945 in Hanoi, soon after the end of the Second World War, Ho Chi Minh, head of the communist nationalist movement the Viet Minh, seized power and decreed the country's independence on behalf of the provisional government, officially proclaiming the birth of the Democratic Republic of Vietnam. Emperor Bao Dai was forced to abdicate.

In North Africa, France had to face a serious crisis which began in Algeria with the uprising of the National Liberation Front in 1954. The war then spread to Morocco and Tunisia and eventually even threatened the French Republic itself. The protectorates of Morocco and Tunisia were granted independence in March 1956 without any armed struggle. Algeria, on the other hand, was considered to be an integral part of France, and events took a different turn. It was only after a painful eight-year-long war, which lasted from the 1954 insurrection to the Évian Accords of March 1962, that Algeria became an independent state.

From 1957 onwards, it was the turn of the former British, French, Belgian and Portuguese possessions in sub-Saharan Africa to gradually gain independence.

England:

The campaigns of civil disobedience led by Gandhi in India during the interwar years had exasperated Great Britain. India, a poor country but one with a large population, intended to play a role on the world stage by making itself the primary advocate of neutralist anti-colonialism. However, at the end of the Second World War the British Government did not have the means to face a new colonial war. It eventually decided to grant independence to the Indian subcontinent in August 1947, but the period was marked by violent clashes between the Hindu and Muslim communities.

While Gandhi and Nehru, the main leaders of the Congress Party, advocated Indian unity, the Muslim League, directed by Ali Jinnah, called for the creation of an independent Muslim state. The violence between the two sides escalated and degenerated into a civil war. In February 1947, the British decided to evacuate the country, and on 15 August 1947 it was partitioned into two independent states: India, with a Hindu majority, and Pakistan, with a Muslim majority. The Republic of India was proclaimed in January 1950, once the constitution had been drawn up, but it remained a member of the British Commonwealth.

In 1948, two other British possessions, Burma and Ceylon, were granted independence, but Malaya had to wait until 1957 before it achieved the same status.

*Britain's optimism, in vain it now seems, that the Commonwealth would provide a vehicle with which it could maintain influence in its former colonies is a clear illustration of London's desire to maintain an informal imperial relationship with its past dependencies. It is therefore difficult to agree with the contention that British decolonization in Africa was voluntary, but rather a reluctant response to the growing pressures of various forces, chief among them **nationalism** and international opinion.*

During the 1960s, England decolonized most of their Africa colonies, off the pressures that Europe faced after WWII, and these fears were the fears that Russia, would respond to the Nationalist dissatisfaction, and the Rooi Gevaar, became the South African political battle plan.

Long Walk to Freedom

IN 1946, a number of critical events occurred that shaped my political development and the direction of the struggle. The mineworkers' strike of 1946, in which 70,000 African miners along the Reef went on strike, affected me greatly. At the initiative of J. B. Marks, Dan Tloome, Gaur Radebe, and a number of ANC labor activists, the African Mine Workers Union (AMWU) had been created in the early 1940s. There were as many as 400,000 African miners working on the Reef, most of them making no more than two shillings a day. The union leadership had repeatedly pressed the Chamber of Mines for a minimum wage of ten shillings a day, as well as family housing and two weeks' paid leave. The chamber ignored the union's demands.

In one of the largest such actions in South African history, the miners went on strike for a week and maintained their solidarity. The state's retaliation was ruthless. The leaders were arrested, the compounds surrounded by police, and the AMWU offices ransacked. A march was brutally repulsed by police; twelve miners died. The Natives Representative Council adjourned in protest. I had a number of relations who were mineworkers, and during the week of the strike I visited them, discussed the issues, and expressed my support.

<u>*Long Walk to Freedom — 1949 Programme of Action:*</u>

The Program of Action approved at the annual conference called for the pursuit of political rights through the use of boycotts, strikes, civil disobedience, and noncooperation. In addition, it called for a national day of work stoppage in protest against the racist and reactionary policies of the government. This was a departure from the days of decorous protest, and many of the old stalwarts of the ANC were to fade away in this new era of greater militancy. Youth League members had now graduated to the senior organization.

We had now guided the ANC to a more radical and revolutionary path.

As you follow my writing, you will become very aware of just how critical I am of Nelson Mandela, the ANC minutes of the December 1949 Congress, shows that Mandela did not attend the 1949 Congress, and the PAC followers will credit Robert Sobukwe for the 1949 Programme of Action.

December 1949, our two *Africanist Nationalist* protagonists, have now guided the ANC to a more radical and revolutionary path, had they remained united, African self-determination should have taken place in 1950, when India were given self-determination, it was a time of stability, a time where our white population would have integrated into the administration and management of the country, but this does not take place.

Nelson Mandela's political philosophy was Africanist Nationalist, as leader of the ANC, when does he change, when did he sell-out.

Our two protagonists needed to be divided, if **'we'** did not want self-determination of the African Nationalist to take place, it did not take place, so logically, there was a 'we' do did not want it to take place.

Was it the English Government who was handing out self-determination all over the world, granted, a manipulated self-determination, or, the Nationalist Party who had surprisingly won the 1948 general election, or was the mining sector, the main obstacle?

The promise of wealth, using the English pound, is the most powerful weapon, that the wealth group, the white capitalist sector, the mining industry, 'Globalization Participants' had to encourage, 'love for the whites', that would allow the white capitalist economy, to survive.

'Love white versus anti-white', is the principle, that protects the white capitalist monopoly today, it divided the Africanist Nationalist of 1949, and maintains the divide today, it is our obstacle to achieving the Brotherhood of Man, in Africa, our obstacle to achieving a social democracy.

History, through our 'new bible', Long Walk to Freedom, confirms that protagonist Nelson Mandela, was the one who elected to move away from the Africanist 1949 Programme of Action, to 'love the whites', to protect the wealth that the whites had extracted from our land, and would continue to extract, however, what the Globalization Participants failed to understand in 1955, is which of our two protagonists, carried the majority African support?

Had Mandela carried the ANC majority support, which in turn would have been the majority of the blacks, and the Macmillan winds of change, February 03, 1960, would have paved the way to handing over to the ANC, under Nelson Mandela, within a year, what the English, and the National Party, were not aware of, was that Mandela did not carry the majority support, and six weeks later, by March 21, 1960, they discovered the support for the Africanist, an extract from the Macmillan speech;

Well you understand this better than anyone, you are sprung from Europe, the home of nationalism, here in Africa you have yourselves created a free nation. A new nation. Indeed in the history of our times yours will be recorded as the first of the African nationalists.

It would take another 34 years, and South Africa would be the last, not the first.

Mangaliso Robert Sobukwe

Our protagonist, Robert Sobukwe, thanks to the media, the politicians, the business people, is never closely looked at. The whites all believe that Robert Sobukwe, was anti-white, that he hated whites, I was never exposed to 'Robert Sobukwe', and today, I believe that, as a white, during the period 1955 to 1961, I should have been given an opportunity, to be exposed to the Sobukwe philosophy, that is still hidden from us today.

Most elderly Black people were Africanist supporters, and today, even the most ardent ANC veteran, will say that the only difference between the ANC and the PAC is as follows;

"The PAC hates the whites, and the ANC love the whites."

This mindset, is the tool that keeps the values of the Africanist hidden, invisible, as the Globalization participants, whether black or white, do not have space in the economy, for a black who does not 'love' the white.

A letter to all the white liberal struggle veterans:

<u>*Dear White Liberal,*</u>

I challenge you to read this Sobukwe inaugural speech, or rather selected extracts, obviously influenced by my biased thoughts, and my wish to focus on South Africa, and then answer to why, your 'liberal' actions in the 1950s, objected to this philosophy;

INTERNATIONAL SCENE

We are living today, Sons and Daughters of the Soil, fighters in the cause of African freedom, we are living today in an era that is pregnant with untold possibilities for both good and evil. In the course of the past two years we have seen man breaking asunder, with dramatic suddenness, the chains that have bound his mind, solving problems which for ages it has been regarded as sacrilege even to attempt to solve. However, in spite of all these rapid advances in the material and physical world, man appears to be either unwilling or unable to solve the problem of social relations between man and man. Because of this failure on the part of man, we see the world split today into two large hostile blocks, the so-called Capitalist and Socialist blocks represented by the U.S.A. and the Soviet Union respectively. These two blocks are engaged in terrible competition, use tough language and tactics, employ brinkmanship stunts which have the whole world heading for a nervous breakdown. They each are armed with terrible weapons of destruction and continue to spend millions of pounds in the production of more and more of these weapons. In spite of all the diplomatic talk of co-existence, these blocks each behave as though they did not believe that co-existence was possible.

AFRIKA'S POSITION

There is again a scramble for Afrika and both the Soviet Union and the United States of America are trying to win the loyalty of the African States. Afrika is being wooed with more ardour than she has ever been.

There is a lot of flirting going on, of course, some Africans [are] flirting with the Soviet camp, and others with the American camp. In some cases the courtship has reached a stage where the parties are going out together; and they probably hold hands in the dark but nowhere has it yet reached a stage where the parties can kiss in public without blushing. This wooing occurs at a time when the whole continent of Afrika is in labour, suffering the pangs of a new birth and everybody is looking anxiously and expectantly towards Afrika to see, as our people so aptly put it ukuthi iyozala nkomoni (what creature will come forth).

We are being wooed internationally at a time when in South Africa, the naked forces of savage Herrenvolkism are running riot; when a determined effort is being made to annihilate the African people through systematic starvation; at a time when brutal attempts are being made to retard, dwarf and stunt the mental development of a whole people through organised "miseducation"; at a time when thousands of our people roam the streets in search of work and are being told by the foreign ruler to go back to a "home" which he has assigned them, whether that means the breakup of their families or not; at a time when the distinctive badge of slavery and humiliation, the "dom pass" is being extended from the African male dog to the African female bitch.

But we must point out that we are not blind to the fact that the countries which pursue a policy of planned state economy have outstripped, in industrial development, those that follow the path of private enterprise. Today, China is industrially far ahead of India. Unfortunately, however, this rapid industrial development has been accompanied in all cases by a rigid totalitarianism notwithstanding Mao Tse Tung's "Hundred Flowers" announcement.

Africanists reject totalitarianism in any form and accept political democracy as understood in the west. We also reject the economic exploitation of the many for the benefit of a few.

We accept as policy the equitable distribution of wealth aiming, as far as I am concerned, to equality of income which to me is the only basis on which the slogan of "equal opportunities" can be founded.

Borrowing then the best from the East and the best from the West we nonetheless retain and maintain our distinctive personality and refuse to be the satraps or stooges of either power block.

THE RACE QUESTION

And now for the thorny questions of race. I do not wish to give a lengthy and learned dissertation on Race. Suffice it to say that even those scientists who do recognise the existence of separate races, have to admit that there are border line cases which will not fit into any of the three Races of mankind. All scientists agree that all men can trace their ancestry back to the first Homo Sapiens, that man is distinguished from other mammals and also from earlier types of man by the nature of his intelligence.

The structure of the body of man provides evidence to prove the biological unity of the human species. All scientists agree that there is no "race" that is superior to another, and there is no "race" that is inferior to others. The Africanists take the view that there is only one race to which we all belong, and that is the human race. In our vocabulary therefore, the word 'race' as applied to man, has no plural form. We do, however, admit the existence of observable physical differences between various groups of people, but these differences are the result of a number of factors, chief among which has been geographical isolation.

In Afrika the myth of race has been propounded and propagated by the imperialists and colonialists from Europe, in order to facilitate and justify their inhuman exploitation of the indigenous people of the land. It is from this myth of race with its attendant claims of cultural superiority that the doctrine of white supremacy stems.

Let me close discussion of this topic by declaring, on behalf of the Africanists, that with UNESCO we hold that "every man is his brother's keeper. For every man is a piece of the continent, a part of the main, because he is involved in mankind".

IN SOUTH AFRIKA

In South Africa we recognise the existence of national groups, which are the result of geographical origin within a certain area as well as a shared historical experience of these groups. The Europeans are a foreign minority group, which has exclusive control of political, economic, social and military power.

It is the dominant group. It is the exploiting group, responsible for the pernicious doctrine of White Supremacy, which has resulted in the humiliation, and degradation of the indigenous African people. It is this group which has dispossessed the African people of their land and with arrogant conceit has set itself up as the "guardians", the "trustees" of the Africans. It is this group which conceives of the African people as a child nation, composed of Boys and Girls, ranging in age from 120 years to one day.

It is this group which, after 300 years, can still state with brazen effrontery that the Native, the Bantu, the Kaffir is still backward and savage etc. But they still want to remain "guardians", "trustees", and what have you, of the African

In short, it is this group which has mismanaged affairs in South Africa just as their kith and kin are mismanaging affairs in Europe. It is from this group that the most rabid race baiters and agitators come. It is members of this group who, whenever they meet in their Parliament, say things, which agitate the hearts of millions of peace-loving Africans. This is the group, which turns out thousands of experts on that new South African Science the Native mind.

Then there is the Indian foreign minority group. This group came to this country not as imperialists or colonialists, but as indentured labourers. In the South African set-up of today, this group is an oppressed minority. But there are some members of this group, the merchant class in particular, who have become tainted with the virus of cultural supremacy and national arrogance. This class identifies itself by and large with the oppressor but, significantly, this is the group, which provides the political leadership of the Indian people in South Africa. And all that the politics of this class have meant up to now is preservation and defence of the sectional interests of the Indian merchant class. The down-trodden, poor "stinking coolies" of Natal who, alone, as a result of the pressure of material conditions, can identify themselves with the indigenous African majority in the struggle to overthrow White supremacy, have not yet produced their leadership. We hope they will do so soon.

The Africans constitute the indigenous group and form the majority of the population. They are the most ruthlessly exploited and are subjected to humiliation, degradation and insult. Now it is our contention that true democracy can be established in South Africa and on the continent as a whole, only when White supremacy has been destroyed. And the illiterate and semi-literate African masses constitute the key and centre and content of any struggle for true democracy in South Africa. And the African people can be organised only under the banner of African nationalism in an All-African Organisation where they will by themselves formulate policies and programmes and decide on the methods of struggle without interference from either so-called left-wing or right-wing groups of the minorities who arrogantly appropriate to themselves the right to plan and think for the Africans.

We wish to emphasise that the freedom of the African means the freedom of all in South Africa, the European included, because only the African can guarantee the establishment of a genuine democracy in which all men will be citizens of a common state and will live and be governed as individuals and not as distinctive sectional groups.

OUR ULTIMATE GOALS

In conclusion, I wish to state that the Africanists do not at all subscribe to the fashionable doctrine of South African exceptionalism. Our contention is that South Africa is an integral part of the indivisible whole that is Afrika.

She cannot solve her problems in isolation from and with utter disregard of the rest of the continent. It is precisely for that reason that we reject both apartheid and so-called multi-racialism as solutions of our socio-economic problems.

Apart from the number of reasons and arguments that can be advanced against apartheid, we take our stand on the principle that Afrika is one and desires to be one and nobody, I repeat, nobody has the right to balkanise our land.

Against multi-racialism we have this objection, that the history of South Africa has fostered group prejudices and antagonisms, and if we have to maintain the same group exclusiveness, parading under the term of multi-racialism, we shall be transporting to the new Afrika these very antagonisms and conflicts.

Further, multi-racialism is in fact a pandering to European bigotry and arrogance. It is a method of safeguarding

white interests, implying as it does, proportional representation irrespective of population figures. In that sense it is a complete negation of democracy.

To us the term "multi-racialism" implies that there are such basic insuperable differences between the various national groups here that the best course is to keep them permanently distinctive in a kind of democratic apartheid.

That to us is racialism multiplied, which probably is what the term truly connotes. We aim, politically, at government of the Africans by the Africans, for the Africans, with everybody who owes his only loyalty to Afrika and who is prepared to accept the democratic rule of an African majority being regarded as an African.

We guarantee no minority rights, because we think in terms of individuals, not groups.

Economically we aim at the rapid extension of industrial development in order to alleviate pressure on the land, which is what progress means in terms of modem society.

We stand committed to a policy guaranteeing the most equitable distribution of wealth. Socially we aim at the full development of the human personality and a ruthless uprooting and outlawing of all forms or manifestations of the racial myth.

To sum it up we stand for an Africanist Socialist Democracy.

Here is a tree rooted in African soil, nourished with waters from the rivers of Afrika. Come and sit under its shade and become, with us, the leaves of the same branch and the branches of the same tree. Sons and Daughters of Afrika, I declare this inaugural convention of the Africanists open.

Mangaliso Robert Sobukwe, April 06, 1959

****

<u>*Dear White Liberal,*</u>

I am concerned, my attitude to the white liberal, indicates that I must be conservative?

****

Trump

The Africanist, or rather, the indigenous people of Africa, are 'invisible' to the rest of the world, whenever Globalization is discussed, except for when our media tells them, that there are things that they must accept, because of this monster 'called' Globalization.

We must all accept it, because it is the 1980s creation, born through the modern communication system that we all love.

When Donald Trump makes a statement that could disturb Globalization, Africa, never features in the conversation, even though 'Globalization' was built off Africa, built off Africa's wealth, commencing with the Slave Trade, the foundation of the Globalization wealth.

The only new player, in the Globalization discussion today, is China, who has become the most powerful voice, challenging Trump, as they protect the wealth that was developed by the Western need for profit, at the expense of their labour.

Why does the rest of the economic world support the Chinese, when Trump makes statements, that threaten to take production back to the USA?

It is because Globalization, masquerading as the 'importers and exporters', the western white Capitalist monopoly, or how they prefer their actions to be referred to today, the 'free market economy', created the Chinese as the 'globalization participant' for the production of their products, closing their eyes to the sweat-shop practices, that is politically no longer acceptable in the rest of the world, in order to increase their profits, and increase their accumulated wealth.

China was given carte blanche by the market place, in the late 1980s, to exploit their labour with a guaranteed purchase and distribution of their goods, by the already established markets, allowing all the Globalization participants to increase their wealth, off the exploited Chinese workers, while the factory workers in the USA and Africa, suffered through unemployment.

Most of those who I interact with, condemn me if I show any support for Donald Trump. The world's minority rights activists, drive the anti-Trump campaign, so successfully, that even my Africanist brothers and sisters, will believe that they should hate Trump, I appreciate their sentiments, as he gives the impression that he hates all blacks.

Why do I celebrate Trump?

Let us have a look at his Free Trade policy statements, and let me remind you, 'free trade' does not exist for the African, in South Africa, if you do not have the money, the permit to trade, you can't even walk the streets of Sandton, without being challenged, by the black security guard.

Donald Trump:

US companies pay high tariffs abroad; let's change that
We must create a level playing field for American companies & workers. Currently, when we ship products out of America, many other countries make us pay very high tariffs and taxes--but when foreign companies ship their products into America, we charge them almost nothing.

Protection will make America strong
For many decades, we've enriched foreign industry at the expense of American industry; subsidized the armies of other countries while allowing for the very sad depletion of our military. We've made other countries

rich while the wealth, strength, and confidence of our country has disappeared over the horizon.

One by one, the factories shuttered and left our shores, with not even a thought about the millions upon millions of American workers left behind. The wealth of our middle class has been redistributed across the entire world. But that is the past.

From this day forward, a new vision will govern our land. From this moment on, it's going to be America First.

Every decision on trade, on taxes, on immigration, on foreign affairs, will be made to benefit American workers and American families.

We must protect our borders from the ravages of other countries making our products, stealing our companies, and destroying our jobs.
Protection will lead to great prosperity and strength.

Two simple rules: buy 'American', and hire 'American'
We will get our people off of welfare and back to work-- rebuilding our country with American hands and American labor. We will follow two simple rules: Buy American and Hire American.

We will seek friendship and goodwill with the nations of the world-- but we do so with the understanding that it is the right of all nations to put their own interests first.

We do not seek to impose our way of life on anyone, but rather to let it shine as an example for everyone to follow.

Many South African Africans, who became unemployed, during the 1980s, when the factories where they worked closed, 'shuttered and left our shores', as described by Trump, believe that it was the white who feared the pending freedom of the blacks, who were fleeing, not the Globalization Participants, sacrificing the job opportunities of our people.

Surely 'Africans', south of the Limpopo, would you not wish for a President of South Africa, to promote the Donald Trump policy, to bring employment and income to our people.

If not, you are a 'Globalization Participant', who make profits off the exploited Chinese, at the expense of the South African unemployed, you do not care, about the poverty unemployed Africans, south of the Limpopo.

****

Origins of Globalization

Globalization originated in the mid 1400s, as the Age of Discovery, drove the European countries efforts to find access to Asia and Africa's mineral and agricultural wealth, the Spice, Opium, Silk, Gold and other mineral wealth, Ivory, and other animal products, controlled by the Arab, African, & Asian communities, with Venice, the link into Europe, generating great wealth.

The New World, the Americas, get 'discovered' in the process, 1492.

Slave Trade:

The use of slaves existed for thousands of years, in order for the miners, the harvesters, to produce and convey their goods to the market, the salves were not necessarily traded as a commodity, until the 1600s.

The term, 'slave trade', becomes one of the many identities, that the Globalization Participants will use, one of the Globalization monster's disguises, that hides their identity, and when it is necessary to do so, the slaves are emancipated, told they are freed, and another name will be allocated, to the new form of subjugation, and the enemy remains hidden, parading in their new disguise.

Globalization, has paraded in different disguises, through till 1985, when communication technology, allowed the evil to be named, when the time comes, it will be changed.

Over the years, Globalization has been disguised as;
Slave Trade,   Colonization,   Apartheid,
and many more disguises are used, and when changes needed to take place, *'emancipation' 'decolonized', 'free market', 'freedom' and democracy* is used, to pacify those that were subjugated, while they remain subjugated.

The Irish Slave Trade:

The Irish Slave Trade is very contentious, the Irish themselves, wishing to avoid their 'slave heritage', however, I include this Google Research article, aimed at the Africanist reader, as it confirms the power of the 'white skin', the fact that, as a white skin, you are accepted, to the extent that, once the 'white slaves' were freed, they were able to integrate into the white capitalist economy, where their African slave brothers and sisters could not. The African slave although freed, remained subjugated, due to the colour of their skin.

Secondly, for all my white brothers and sisters who would like to accuse the African Chiefs for selling their 'people' into slavery, you should take note of the Irish Slave heritage.

In the GlobalResearch article below (Part IV of a five part series), **Liam Hogan** *reviews the data and presents an analysis of the literature.*

The Irish slave trade began when 30,000 Irish prisoners were sold as slaves to the New World. The King James I Proclamation of 1625 required Irish political prisoners be sent overseas and sold to English settlers in the West Indies. By the mid 1600s, the Irish were the main slaves sold to Antigua and Montserrat. At that time, 70% of the total population of Montserrat were Irish slaves.

Ireland quickly became the biggest source of human livestock for English merchants. The majority of the early slaves to the New World were actually white.

From 1641 to 1652, over 500,000 Irish were killed by the English and another 300,000 were sold as slaves. Ireland's population fell from about 1,500,000 to 600,000 in one single decade. Families were ripped apart as the British did not allow Irish dads to take their wives and children with them across the Atlantic. This led to a helpless population of homeless women and children. Britain's solution was to auction them off as well.

During the 1650s, over 100,000 Irish children between the ages of 10 and 14 were taken from their parents and sold as slaves in the West Indies, Virginia and New England. In this decade, 52,000 Irish (mostly women and children) were sold to Barbados and Virginia. Another

30,000 Irish men and women were also transported and sold to the highest bidder. In 1656, Cromwell ordered that 2000 Irish children be taken to Jamaica and sold as slaves to English settlers.

Many people today will avoid calling the Irish slaves what they truly were: Slaves. They'll come up with terms like "Indentured Servants" to describe what occurred to the Irish. However, in most cases from the 17th and 18th centuries, Irish slaves were nothing more than human cattle.

As an example, the African slave trade was just beginning during this same period. It is well recorded that African slaves, not tainted with the stain of the hated Catholic theology and more expensive to purchase, were often treated far better than their Irish counterparts.

African slaves were very expensive during the late 1600s (50 Sterling). Irish slaves came cheap (no more than 5 Sterling). If a planter whipped or branded or beat an Irish slave to death, it was never a crime. A death was a monetary setback, but far cheaper than killing a more expensive African. The English masters quickly began breeding the Irish women for both their own personal pleasure and for greater profit. Children of slaves were themselves slaves, which increased the size of the master's free workforce. Even if an Irish woman somehow obtained her freedom, her kids would remain slaves of her master. Thus, Irish moms, even with this new found emancipation, would seldom abandon their kids and would remain in servitude.

In time, the English thought of a better way to use these women (in many cases, girls as young as 12) to increase their market share: The settlers began to breed

Irish women and girls with African men to produce slaves with a distinct complexion. These new "mulatto" slaves brought a higher price than Irish livestock and, likewise, enabled the settlers to save money rather than purchase new African slaves. This practice of interbreeding Irish females with African men went on for several decades and was so widespread that, in 1681, legislation was passed "forbidding the practice of mating Irish slave women to African slave men for the purpose of producing slaves for sale." In short, it was stopped only because it interfered with the profits of a large slave transport company.

England continued to ship tens of thousands of Irish slaves for more than a century. Records state that, after the 1798 Irish Rebellion, thousands of Irish slaves were sold to both America and Australia. There were horrible abuses of both African and Irish captives. One British ship even dumped 1,302 slaves into the Atlantic Ocean so that the crew would have plenty of food to eat.

Another interesting observation, is that when reasons for colonization are discussed today, they give credit to the 'social' need, for Colonization; bunkum!

As a result of industrialization, major social problems grew in Europe: unemployment, poverty, homelessness, social displacement from rural areas, and so on. These social problems developed partly because not all people could be absorbed by the new capitalist industries. One way to resolve this problem was to acquire colonies and export this "surplus population." This led to the establishment of settler-colonies in Algeria, Tunisia, South Africa, Namibia, Angola, Mozambique, and central

African areas like Zimbabwe and Zambia. Eventually the overriding economic factors led to the colonization of other parts of Africa.

Kaalvoet Comment:

If it was a major social problem in Europe, their surplus population would have arrived in Africa and Australia, as a 'refugee' seeking assistance from the African, not to subjugate them.

Globalization in picture form:

Hidden in the Slave Trade discussion, is the wealth of the world, the Dutch East Indies Company, the English East Indies Company, and other wealthy families, who were the investors and shareholders, in the shipping from the Age of Discovery, the importers & exporters, the first leg of the triangle, the slave trade from Africa to the New World, was not the only element for generating wealth, the second leg of the triangle, was the New World agricultural production, moved to the Europe market, and as their wealth grew, the building and mining equipment, moved from Europe to Africa, was the third leg of the Triangle, the completion of what is Globalization.

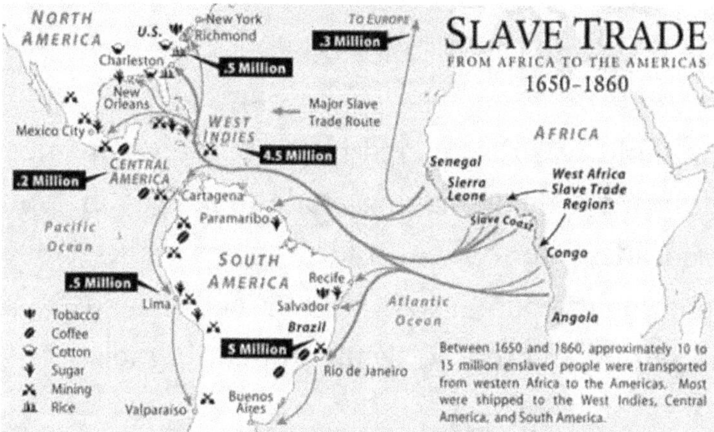

Africa - South of the Limpopo;

Diamonds (1867), Xhosa (1879), Zulu (1879) Gold (1886), Land (1888) Africa Colonized, except for the two Boer Republics (1888), Boer defeated (1902), Union of South Africa (1910), so Africa, south of the Limpopo was Colonised, the Globalization industry, as depicted in the slave trade picture above, entrenched.

The 'wealth of the world', invested heavily in the shipping industry, effectively becoming the importers and exporters of the world, or as they would like to be referred to today, the 'Global Market'.

These importers and exporters, made their wealth from Silk, Spices, Cocaine, Slaves, Tobacco, Sugar, Coke, Gold, plus other products. They moved slaves to the New World, Agricultural products from the New

World to Europe, and then mining and building equipment from Europe to Africa.

When Gold was discovered in 1886, the companies and wealthy individuals, having made their wealth from the slave trade, the opium trade, spices, silks, tobacco, cotton, sugar, 'purchased' large tracts of land from the ZARepublic, in order to secure mineral rights.

During 1878, very little land had been surveyed and owned, and when the 'Anglo American' buys the land to secure the mineral rights, the African farmers become sharecroppers, and the Boer becomes a 'Bywooner', both tenants on their own land, not only paying rental to the new landowner, but for the next 50 years, clearing and developing the lands.

Suddenly the African clans, where they had been farming for years, found the white landowner, carrying a piece of paper, and threatening to evict them, if they did not pay rental.

The African farmer, having developed his lands, elected to pay the 50% of his crop, to the landowner, for permission to continue farming, the African farmer, becoming a sharecropper, on his own farm.

The Afrikaner, the Boer, had not been on the land for the same period of time, but on the land that they were farming, they were faced with the same landowner, and the threat of eviction if they did not pay rental, the Afrikaner farmer, becoming a 'bywooner' on his own farm.

The Globalization Participants, stole the land and mineral rights, from those farmers who were farming on the land, when they bought the land from the ZAR, both black, soon to become sharecroppers, and white, soon to become bywooners, paying the holder of the 'title deed' to continue farming on the land that they had established and tilled.

On March 15, 2018, on one of Radio 702 morning shows, a white female caller confirms this to Eusebius McKaiser, her comment goes as follows;

> *"In 1880, my parents bought a farm in the Transvaal, they were too old to farm, so they leased their farm out for twenty years, when the lease expired, that had done well, the farm was developed, and virtually paid."*

To the 702 caller, you are celebrated because you tell the presenter that you will not leave and go to Australia, you should not have the pride that you have for the success of your parents, the farms bought in the 1880s, were bought to secure the mineral rights, the sharecropper and the bywooner, were your tenants, and through their hard work, they paid for this white Colonial heritage.

No English speaking white 'farmer' would have purchased land, in the Transvaal, in 1880, for any reason, other than mineral rights.

To the 702 caller and presenter Eusebius McKaiser , this system of farming, throughout Africa, was commonly referred to a Kaffir Farming, the 'white farmer', was not farming with crops, rather with African people, that brought them their additional wealth.

The black sharecrop farmer, was the preferred tenant, he worked with his entire family clan, whereas, the Boer did not have this family working ethic. In order to make the celebrated 702 caller wealthy, the tax system encouraged the black farmers to work on white owned land, tax was levied at £3 if living on Native territory, £2 if living on government controlled land, and only £1, if living on white owned land.

In order to secure control over the mineral wealth, the English find reason to go to war against the Boer Republics, the war is savage, the scorched earth policy, removing the Boer's cattle, burning their crops, burning their homes, and taking their woman and children into concentration camps, *dear Queen Elizabeth*, this must rate as the English Coloniser's lowest point in South Africa, but then, not to those who benefitted.

What we do not realise, is that the blacks we removed from the lands during this scorched earth policy, were not Boer farm labourers, they were farmers, and the cattle we removed from them, was their wealth, the crops we burnt, was their food, and the homes we burnt, was their family homes.

After the Anglo Boer War, the black farmers were able to reestablish, their family farming operations, quicker than the Boer, and thus, many young Boers remained landless. The better black farmers, many of them, as a family unit, more productive than the Boer, were kept on the 'wealth of the world's' land, till 1930 to 1936.

This process takes place, as the mining industry grows, the manufacturing and service industry alongside, the railroads, the roads, and infrastructure, as the City of Johannesburg rises from the bare ground, and Africans are the main supply of labour. As this takes place, the numbers of people requiring food in Johannesburg and the mining areas rockets, and as the African farmer is the only farmer planting cereal crops, they sell to the employers, some earning anything between £100 to £500 per annum, after paying 50% of their crop as a rent.

This when you could buy a plot in Eloff Street, Johannesburg for £5.

The African farmer was the preferred farmer, due to the production that a family unit was able to produce. The Boer did not plant maize and other cereal products, as they could not sell into the African consumer market.

Between 1910 and 1914, the system wrote a book, MAIZE, a TEXT-BOOK[5], aimed at encouraging the Boer to start planting Maize, A few relevant extracts are included.

Chapter 1, Page 2.
Maize is one of the easiest crops to grow, standing more rough usage than perhaps any other; a favourite Kaffir method of planting is to scatter the seed broadcast over the unbroken veldt and then plough the ground; even with this crude treatment crops of 1,5 to 2 muids of grain per acre obtained.

---

[5] https://archive.org/stream/maizeitshistoryc00burt#page/808/mode/2up

Chapter 1, Page 3-4

We still hear South African farmers say that maize is a Kaffir crop, and that maize-growing does not pay the more ambitious white farmer. We hope to show in the following pages that, except where abnormal economic or unfavourable climatic conditions prevail, this is not the case when the crop is grown properly.

What the American Farmer Thinks of It. - In view of the fact that the United States produces 820,000,000 muids of maize per annum - three quarters of the world's crop, and that this is not grown with cheap "native" labour, it may be well to look for a moment at the attitude of the American farmers towards the maize crop.
In the United States it is a common saying that "Corn is King". "Corn" in America is maize.

Chapter 1, Page 5.
Maize is a White Man's Crop. - Maize is essentially a white man's crop, and Prof. Carver (1) doubts whether it "could be grown at all, as it is grown in the Corn-belt, if dependence had to be placed upon Negro labour". The labour employed in that part of the country is entirely white, earning about £5 per month and board the year round. Yet ....

Chapter 1, Page 7.
Future Possibilities of Development in South Africa, - European corn brokers have recently referred to South Africa as the future maize granary of Europe. Maize will always be the staple cash crop of South Africa. As its value for stock food becomes better appreciated, the local demand will increase, and in this connection Earl Grey's recent prophecy of a shortage in the world's beef supply is suggestive. At the present time the country has only begun to show that it is possible to produce good maize. The traveller is impressed with the enormous areas of fertile land, suitable for growing maize, which are at present untouched by the plough, virgin sod like the American prairies. …………

Driving this initiative is the Export market and the perceived unreliability of our black farmers.

This book was published in 1914, it would have been prepared before 1913, nowhere in this publication do the writers allow for black participation in the agricultural economy, even though the 1913 Native Land Act was only just actioned.

During the period 1910 to 1913 the blacks purchased 78 farms, 300 000 ha. and paid 95 000 pounds, triggering another threat of the economic invasion of the white economy, triggering the 1913 Native Land Act.

Note, effectively, the purchasers of the crops and livestock, are their landlords, who deduct their share from the crop, but as the requirements escalate, so the African farmers, clear and till more land, all in the benefit of the landowner, and the African farmer, driven by the desire to buy his own land, works harder, bring wealth to his landowner.

WallStreet collapses October 1929.

In October 1929, WallStreet collapses, the depression hits the world, and the second leg of the shipping industry collapses, the new world unable to provide agricultural supplies into Europe, the South African 1880s 'land owners', turn to their own land, to supplement Europe's needs, or rather, the loss of profits from the new world agricultural sector.

When WallStreet collapses, the Globalization that had existed for nearly 300 years, collapses, the financial uncertainty, causes the Americans to reduce input, crops are not planted, and the second leg of the triangle collapses.

At this stage these land owners, these importers and exporters, these investors, make a decision that they can't trust the black farmer to provide the volume and quality needed, *it is quoted that they were concerned that the black farmer would sell his crop to another for a hand full of beads, and when he has enough money, he would sit under a tree and drink beer till hungry.*

The 'wealth of the world' sub-divided their 'stolen' land, the land south of the Limpopo, paid for through the sweat of the sharecropper and bywooner, that over the years the sharecropper and bywooner had cleared and tilled, sub-dividing their land, and selling off to young white Afrikaner farmers, bringing with their land, the equipment, the seed, fertiliser, and training, launching the Compound Interest funding.

By now the 1913 Native Land Act is in place, they are unable to sell to the African, not that I believe they ever would have.

The success of the young Boer, and the structure that developed them into the power that they are today, was that the 'importers and exporters' undertook to buy all their crop and livestock production, they created the storage and transport systems, the milling and distributions facilities.

Off this arrangement, the 'Global Market' developed, the blacks were forced into their cages, and were forced to buy the grade of food, that was not suitable for export, and then, the very white, very fine, maize meal that was to become the 'African' meal.

The 'importers & exporters, needing to fill the Americas crops into Europe, selected the best quality and exported to Europe, their next basket that they already controlled, was the supply of cereal crops into the labour sector, and the new market that opened up, was the Africans, now all removed from productive land, needing to provide labour, in order to purchase their staple foods from the 'importer and exporter'?

Right at this stage, the French West Africa farmers, suffer severe losses, as the production south of the Limpopo, causes prices in French West Africa to plummet.

As we move through the 1936 to 1943 period, the Americas are back in full production thanks to the WWII needs, and with the excess of cereal crops being produced, the globalization industry, as we know it is born.

Maize, or as known in the Americas, Corn, is being overproduced, the 'importers & exporters', take the

Corn-flake, a health flake, add a bit of sugar, and their media marketing, and soon the world is fed the 'Corn-Flake' as the 'must' eat breakfast.

Throughout the world, throughout Africa, the conglomerates start to control the milling industry, soon the small grocer will disappear, and the super-market, to be controlled by the Globalisation industry, dictates what we eat, what we drink, what we wear, and what we drive.

If we had not removed the African from the farming activity, they would still be controlling the food chain in Africa today.

If South Africa wishes to become a nation that does not need the *constable,* we need to focus our land expropriation and land reform on the farming entities that were build on the wealth of the mining industry.

In the next Chapter '*Kwashiorkor*' the English remove the African from their lands, restrict their production of Maize, and then, develop the very fine, very white maize, that brings the Globalization market, greater profits, linked to the USA supply into Europe.

This is a message from His Master's Voice;

"All this was done many years ago, and it was all done in the indigenous black persons interest."

I quote from 'Capital & Labour in South Africa' - By Du Toit;

The Council of SABRA[6] noted with concern the large measure of the integration of natives into the white economy, and is convinced that if this situation is allowed to continue, and develop further, it must necessarily have disastrous consequences for the whites, as well as the natives.

The council therefore pleads for the consistent application of the policy of separate development as the only satisfactory measure.

*****

------

[6] *South African Bureau of Race relations?*

<u>Kwashiorkor</u>

Kwashiorkor: a form of malnutrition caused by protein deficiency in the diet.

As a white South African, late 1960s, I was very aware that young black children were suffering from Kwashiorkor, the many pictures that filled our media, were shocking, but there was very little concern for the children, or what caused the illness.

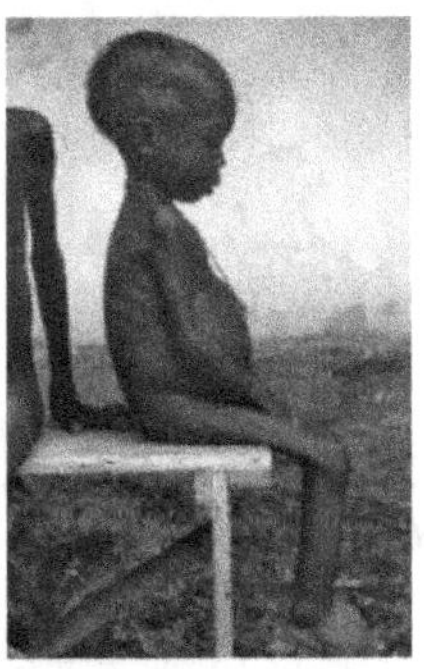

In recent years, as I increased my level of activism, I became of the opinion that part of the problem, was the introduction and marketing of the very fine, very white, maize meal, as a brand to our African population.

In my limited opinion, and the this could only be achieved, if the millers removed the germ and the pericarp, should the food scientists, and the milling industry, have a different perspective, it would be welcome.

We then fed the resulting, very white, very fine, maize meal to our indigenous population, and my limited knowledge, suggests that the germ oil would be extracted, and the bulk of the removed portion, would be used as a supplement to the cattle feed, adding to the profits of the Globalization millers.

I would suggest that, it took the millers a number of years to consider whether the removal of the germ and pericarp, contributed towards the Kwashiorkor illnesses, and decided to add supplements, to the very white, very fine, maize meal, consumed by the African, rater than to put the germ and pericarp, back into the diet.

I do believe that the USA, also fed the very fine maize as a cereal at some stage, but today, their fine maize, is no longer used as a 'porridge', but for a mix in baking muffins and other baked products, they use 'regular corn', their 'grits', and the USA government, school feeding schemes, provide the buy only 'regular corn'.

Having said the above, hopefully we stimulate a food scientist's interest into looking at the problem, I wish to present a Wikipedia blog on production of maize in Kenya, for two reasons, it confirms the intent of the Coloniser with regard to removing the germ and pericarp, while gives South Africans insight into the

English attitude and mindset, that would have guided the Afrikaner, in the process of keeping our Africans subjugated.

Wikipedia:

The Adoption of Maize in Kenya occurred during the British occupation, from the late 19th century through to 1963. In fact, until the 1920s, most of the maize produced by European settlers in Kenya was exported, not eaten domestically. This article tells the story of how maize became the main staple in Kenya.

Introduction of Maize

Prior to the British conquest, the Portuguese had already introduced maize to the coast, where it became common among the Swahili traders. Kenyans incorporated it into their mixed plots and Swidden systems.

Preference for White Maize

Ironically, the preferences of today's African consumers for white as opposed to yellow grain colour began with the influence of the British starch market during these years."
That is because North American producers of yellow maize had a "decisive transportation cost advantage" in supplying Britain.

As early as 1911, producers in Kenya found there was a price premium for white maize. "Though both white and yellow maize varieties of maize were grown, settler farmers were informed by the Secretary of the London Corn Exchange that exports required better grading and uniformity. Farmers discovered that when yellow and white maize were grown in close proximity and cross-pollinated, the grains of the progeny were mixed in colour, rendering it unsuitable for export.

Kaalvoet Comment on Globalization

The USA was able to ship Yellow maize, for animal feed into Europe cheaper than it cost from Kenya to Europe, and, so the Secretary of the London Corn Exchange, advised the Kenyan settlers to concentrate on the White Maize product.

Adoption of Maize as a Staple by Kenyans

During the British occupation of Kenya, the domestic demand for maize grew as Africans left their farms to work on settler farms, in mines or industrial plants, particularly in Kenya, Zambia and Zimbabwe.

Food consumption preferences were influenced by the rations that employers used as in-kind payments. Diets adapted as "people got used to what they consumed".

In the early part of the twentieth century, British settlers started growing maize in larger quantities, and colonial landowners used maize, a cheap food source, as the main form of sustenance for their African farm labourers.

During the period from 1900-25, maize gradually became a staple food in the Kenyan diet, which was previously dominated by the millets, tubers, legumes, and kales commonly found in traditional farming systems.

For urban populations, maize "received a boost" (over native millet and sorghum) in the 1920s with the introduction of the hammer mill. Hammer mills gave a processing cost advantage to maize over small grains, since maize could be dumped into the hopper for grinding, while millet and sorghum husks required de-hulling first.

The prevalence of large-scale, industrial processors in Kenya, Zambia and Zimbabwe contributed to preferences, particularly in urban areas, for dent types. *The removal of the germ and pericarp makes refined meal look whiter, last longer, and taste sweeter than whole meal.* Hammer-milled, whole meal remains the primary staple food in the grain self-sufficient rural areas of these countries.

Marketing Boards

When African farmers began competing with British farmers in growing and selling maize, the white settler farmers successfully lobbied for legislation. In Kenya, the Native Produce Ordinance was passed in 1935. ***Similar laws were passed in other British-controlled African colonies.***

These marketing acts

(1) created state crop-buying stations in European farming areas without parallel investments in African farming areas;

(2) enforced a two-tiered pricing scheme with higher prices for settler farmers than for native Africans; and

(3) established restrictions on grain movement from African areas to towns, mines and other demand centres.

From 1935, the combination of maize legislation, land evictions, and fiscal policies weakened Africans' position in food marketing relative to that of settler farmers in Kenya.

Along with centralised, state maize marketing boards came large-scale grain milling operations.

By the 1950s, Kenyan grain millers began using roller mill technology, producing a "refined and

more expensive type of meal" and giving them "a de facto monopoly on maize meal sales to cities and grain-deficit rural areas once local supplies were exhausted."

As a result of the market regulation, "Settler maize production expanded and producers earned prices that generally exceeded export parity."

Kaalvoet Comment:

On pages 65 to 67 above, I summarise the removal of the African farmer from the white economy, and how, the young white Boer, Afrikaner settler, was put into place by the Globalization participants, how they who stole our land, used the Boer, to secure and to entrench, the power and wealth of the Globalization participants, off the State owned crop-buying stations.

The African in South Africa, will be able to read the subjugation and abuse suffered by their parents and grandparents, from the Kenyan article, and I ask if there was an African Colony, where, this did not take place, in the Colonisation process, or more correctly, the Globalization process?

*****

Mining Industry the Apartheid Architect

Kaalvoet believes that the mining industry, was the architect of Apartheid, and the influence that controlled separate development through to 1994, and beyond, this is confirmed by Anglo American SA, they stop investing when Jacob Zuma becomes ANC President, and the promises to reinvest, when their man, Cyril Ramaphosa, takes control of their selected 'tribe' again, their ANC.

After the Anglo Boer War, 1902, the mines had just started operating, when one morning, nearly forty-thousand men under Roberts moved into Johannesburg. The blacks on the streets celebrated, they tore up their Republican passes that had been issued, accepting that the defeat of the war, would bring them the rewards, that Chamberlain had used to justify the war.

"Because of the 'brutal and disgraceful' treatment of the black population," part of their motivation

Within a week, that very same army that had come to liberate them, instituted the validity of the old 'Pass Law', re-established the old Republican mine police, the courts, and changed the Fort back into a jail, to hold those blacks that did not comply, aimed at keeping the blacks off the streets, forcing them into work, forcing them to build rail-lines, to bring coal to the mines, and move their exports to the sea.

During 1902, the birth of influx and job control regulations, started, with old Transvaal the first to be forced to comply. The Native Affairs Department, established off the base of the Labour Recruitment agents, that had been providing mine labour from Mozambique, through the Kruger Park routes.

The mining industry used the reward system, commissions paid, which turned the labour supply into big business. Gifts and rewards paid to various Chiefs and Commissioners, increased the flow of labour into the Johannesburg area, the mines were faced with many labourers arriving directly, and not through a labour broker. This created unhappiness from the labour brokers, so structures and Native Commissioners, were put in place to avoid conflict.

The Transvaal Province was divided into five labour areas, controlled by five Native Commissioners, charged with control of their people, as they established a system for the administration of justice, so that the new state could control the blacks on the land. Sub-commissioners attended to collection of taxes, issuing of passes, signing labour contracts, and some two hundred poorly paid

Native policemen would ensure compliance. The mining industry, were using the Colonial government to control the black people's movements.

The registration and pass laws, restricting the movement of black people was in place in 1903, 'Apartheid', and separate development, established in order to protect the huge profit potential, that the mining industry was generating, by using 'controlled labour' which had started with the Mozambicans, enslaved by their Portuguese coloniser from 1450s, and then England pulled the British Protectorates into the labour-pool, followed by other African Colonies, resulting in a ***foreign labour contingent of 54% of the total labour force for 150 years.***

These labourers, like the indentured Indians, were brought into our country because our labour was deemed to be too expensive.

During 1870, according to Lieutenant Cunynghame, in his book, 'My Command in South Africa', our male labour were charging 7 English shillings per day for their labour, our woman 5 English shillings per day, while in Suffolk England, a white labourer would be locked out, if he even thought about asking for more than 13 shillings per week.

Importantly, we need to absorb into our minds, this value that the African male had attached to his worth, the 7 English shillings per day rate, would be about £6 pound per month, or, £72 per annum.

The indentured Indian labour was only paid £2 per month, £24 per annum, and this was far more than they were able to earn in India, so there was no shortage of supply.

Let us just divert to why I accuse the mines of using controlled slave labour to ensure profits.
"During 1921, the daily mine wage was 26.1 penny per shift."
"During 1930, the daily mine wage was 25.7 penny per shift."
"During 1936, the daily mine wage was 27.0 penny per shift."

Over fifteen years, the annual mine wage increased from £30.08.00 per annum, to £31.12.00s per annum, an increase of 0,027% per annum.

The Municipalities in Transvaal, Orange Free State, and Natal were paying £32.10.00, only 4% more than the mines.

Note, in 1936, the mines are paying, £31.12.00s per annum, when, in 1870, some 66 years earlier, the African in the Eastern Cape, attached a value to his labour, at £72 per annum.

Using the cheapest labour that could be sourced in Southern and Central Africa, the mining industry and their investors not only exploited the mineral wealth of the country, but, through the lack of allowing open, free participation, they have severely impacted on our still subjugated communities in 2018.

****

1940, during WWII, the Western European powers are faced with the German / Nazi issues, and the Russian, communist threat, the Red Danger, / 'Rooi Gevaar', and the Globalization Participants needed to protect their wealth from the communists, by making sure, that the Africanist Nationalists do not take control of South Africa, as they would move towards the Russians for support, and their wealth, still not extracted from the mines, would move into the hands of the Communist.

Rooi Gevaar, soon becomes Swart Gevaar, for no other reason, than the concept fed to us, is that the blacks would hand South Africa's minerals to the Communist.

As a white, born in 1947, in a poor neighbourhood, even though a neighbour to Sophiatown, I saw very few black people, till 1959, when I started high school, in the east of Johannesburg, and needed to commute daily.

The description 'Swart Gevaar', was an undertone, that rang through the neighbourhood, and when we asked about it, there was no fear for the black person, but a fear that we should never allow the blacks to take control of 'our' country, because they would give the gold and diamonds to the communist, the 'Rooi Gevaar'.

The origins of the fear of the Communist, was the taking over our mineral wealth, the 'Rooi Gevaar', the development of the African Nationalism was feared by the mining industry, so the 'Rooi Gevaar', becomes the 'Swart Gevaar', a call to the white South Africans, to protect the Mining Industry, and as time moves on, the 'Swart Gevaar', extends into a fear, that is still part of South African life today, and subconsciously, dictates the minds of the media, and every tourism participants, as our tourism industry, protects the tourists from the blacks, and keeps white South Africans, separated from the black community.

*****

<u>*The DRC Independence:*</u>

Kaalvoet introduces a brief look at DRC Independence, and the resulting conflict as the wealth of the DRC,

Katanga, becomes a conflict zone, as the USA and Belgium, protect their wealth, from the 'Rooi Gevaar'. Extracted from historyworld.net[7]

On July 11, 1961, Moise Tshombe takes advantage of the collapse of government control. He declares the independence of Katanga. With the help of Belgian troops he is able to expel all units of the Congolese army. The ingredients for the next stage of the Congo's agony are all in place.

With many in the west showing signs of support for Tshombe (mindful of the wealth of his region), Lumumba raises the stakes by asking for Soviet help in recovering Katanga. During August there arrive from Russia aircraft, arms, technicians and military advisers.

Within two months of independence the Congo has become a potential flashpoint of the Cold War. The issue dominates debate in the general assembly of the UN. Meanwhile UN forces are on the ground trying to hold the peace. In the event a local coup, still during the first three months of independence, proves a turning point.

---

[7] http://www.historyworld.net/wrldhis/PlainTextHistories.asp?historyid=ad34

On September 4 President Kasavubu announces that he has dismissed Lumumba as prime minister. Lumumba, in response, hurries to the radio station to broadcast that he has dismissed Kasavubu as president. The resulting confusion is only resolved when the 29-year-old minister of defence, Mobutu Sese Seko, declares on September 14 that he is 'neutralizing' all politicians and is temporarily taking over the duties of government in the name of the army.

Mobutu is secretly in Kasavubu's camp (both act with the encouragement of the CIA, alarmed by Lumumba's Soviet policy). One of his first actions is to close down the Soviet embassy. In February 1961 he returns the government to Kasavubu, who appoints him commander of the army.

Meanwhile Lumumba has been murdered, in circumstances which remain mysterious. In November 1960 he unwisely leaves Léopoldville, where he has been living under UN protection. He is captured by forces loyal to Kasavubu and is sent in January 1961 - presumably with only one purpose in mind - to Katanga.

He is last seen on arrival in Katanga being transferred, blindfold and handcuffed, from the plane to a waiting car. No more is heard of him.

He is believed to have been murdered either by Katangan police or Belgian mercenaries. Evidence emerges years later to suggest that both President Eisenhower and the Belgian government were party to plans to eliminate this left-wing African leader.

****

By 1940, the mining industry reached a new high, employing three hundred and sixty-thousand labourers, with South Africa Eastern Cape, the Mfengu Thembu base, providing the complement with one hundred and twenty-thousand of their young men

Had the mining industry, used only South African labour in their total labour force, and paid them maybe 60% of their 'own labour value', South Africa as a nation, would be wealthier today, both black and white, and the country, but the Rand Lords and the mining investors, would not have extracted the wealth that they did from us?

This would have caused ownership of the mineral wealth being transferred to the people, and 'Swart Gevaar', would have been removed, as 'Rooi Gevaar' no longer existed.

Let us have a look at the labour trends and the motivations for change?

See 1940 to 1949, f to g, on Chart 1 below:

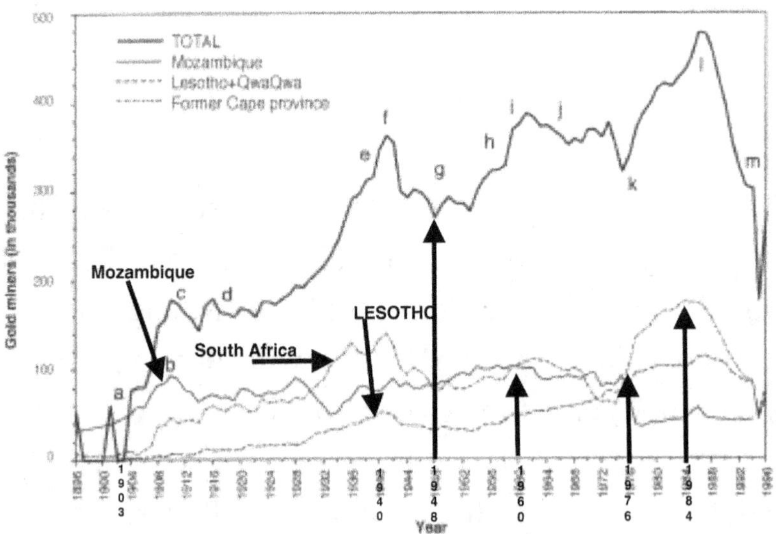

Kaalvoet Observations:

There is little doubt that the restriction on the movement of black people was to hide, the use of the cheap slave labour used in the mines for 150 years. Imagine the chaos if my black brothers could move freely in large numbers, and discover that the mine labour was mainly foreign nationals.

During the period 1940 to 1946, the South African labour complement dropped, from 120 000, to 70 000, was it the labourers that did not want to work, or the mining industries reaction to the Africanist Nationalism, and strikes, that was developing in South Africa?

Not sure whether my Afrikaans NP brothers, are going to smile about the next observation, but based on the 1940 to 1948 situation as reflected in the labour picture, Chart 1, I am of the opinion that the mining industry influenced the 1948 elections, stimulating the Swart Gevaar, putting the NP and the Afrikaner into power, leaving the responsibility of controlling the labour force, to the Afrikaner.

Of importance here, and why I am of the opinion that the English, the Anglo American, influenced the 1948 elections in the favour of the National Party, dates back to the Africanist Nationalism that was uniting Africa during WWII, the Africans participated in the Coloniser's armed forces, and underlying their motivation to support the Coloniser, was the undertakings by the Coloniser, to address the subjugation suffered by the Africans, when the war was over.

The English wished to avoid this situation, and the easiest method, was to change the face of their subjugators.

Nelson Mandela, driving the Africanist Nationalist direction towards the 1949 Programme, confirms my theory that the Nationalist Party was a surprise victor in the 1948 general election.

Long Walk to Freedom

The victory was a shock. The United Party and General Smuts had beaten the Nazis, and surely they would defeat the National Party. On election day, I attended a meeting in Johannesburg with Oliver Tambo and several others. We barely discussed the question of a Nationalist government because we did not expect one. The meeting went on all night and we emerged at dawn and found a newspaper vendor selling the Rand Daily Mail: the Nationalists had triumphed. I was stunned and dismayed, but Oliver took a more considered line. "I like this," he said. "I like this." I could not imagine why. He explained, "Now we will know exactly who our enemies are and where we stand."

I am of the opinion that, the 'Anglo American' investors using foreign labour to extract maximum profits from the gold mines, could not allow 'freedom of movement' for the black South Africans, influx control and passes were essential, to maintain the mining industry.

Off this principle, I am of the opinion that the 1948 general election, was manipulated to transfer power to the Afrikaner, who had Anglicised leaders, who would do the bidding of his Master's Voice, for a few 'pounds', and recognition, by the Queen.

These Anglicised NP leader, would be influenced by the white capitalist monopoly, to do their every bidding, and unfortunately, they had a community, struggling to recover from the Anglo Boer War, and ten years of depression, plus two World Wars, so the police and military, young men all skilled in using weapons, would obey all instructions, to protect the 'wealth' of the country.

The Sharpeville Massacre, took place, with or without direct instruction, in order to protect his Master's Wealth, and then the Master, encouraged the May 31, 1961, Republic of South Africa, deceleration, to finally transfer the sins of the Master, to the Afrikaner

The Kaalvoet theory sounds crazy, so let us have a look at the Anglo American 2018 scenario:

Anglo American and the mining industries.

In Kaalvoet's opinion, this industry was responsible for Apartheid, and who would rule the country, having first selected the NP to protect their wealth extraction in 1948, as the 1943 Bill of Rights developed into African Nationalism by the Africans in South Africa, the Mining

Industry, selected Nelson Mandela and the ANC, as their preferred partners, when needed.

In general, the majority of the South African black labour was sent to the mines from the Transkei, what part did the mining industry play in the establishment of the Bantustans, from 1974, mine labour was recruited, or allocated to the various Bantustans, it obviously was a decision, aimed at supporting the NP government, or did the English Coloniser drive the 'division' of the labour force.

Monday, September 03, 1984, South Africa's new constitution creating the tricameral parliament became effective, the day that South Africa's first executive state president took the oath of office. The Vaal Triangle exploded into a 'smouldering human rage', lasting through to 1994, rage that would cripple our country, and leaves the scars behind today.

Kaalvoet sees the reduction of labour as depicted on the chart 1, as the mining industries decision to mechanise, to remove the need to too many black workers, while the labour complement reduces by 66,6%, the value of the output between 1985 to 2000, increased by more than 250%.

South Africa went into the transition to ANC leadership, without debriefing, without preparation, the blacks were not prepared, and less so the whites. Early 1994, when the angry youth had agreed to lay down their weapons, maybe, we needed another two years of preparation?

Jacob Zuma was not part of the Mining Industry selected ANC leaders, and thus the anti-Jacob Zuma campaign by the Country, when he came into power. This is confirmed by Anglo American, as they contribute to restoring their selected ANC, under President Ramaphosa.

MINING INDABA   KEYNOTE ADDRESS

Norman Mbazima, Deputy Chairman of Anglo American SA
5 February 2018

o   In December last year, the South African Chamber of Mines published a report on mining investment in South Africa, which shows that:

*   Gross fixed investment in mining has been stagnant since 2009, and has declined by 5% over the course of the last three years;
*   While net investment has declined by 57% since 2008;

* And despite commodity prices improving by about 11% on average since 2006, our output as an industry has been stagnant;

o I want to argue—and I hope I am preaching to the converted here—that we urgently need to get investment back on the agenda for South Africa.

o In this regard, it was encouraging to see how the internal rules and processes of the African National Congress, South Africa's governing party, were observed even during a hotly contested elective conference last December. This resulted in a credible outcome, which we think is a significant 'first step' towards stabilising the political dynamics in our country.

o As the country prepares for its 5th democratic election, which will be held next year, we look forward to an exciting period of debate and democratic contestation.

o Our view is that if the right choices are made, South Africa will regain its momentum and this will bring together all social partners—government, business, labour, and civil society—and provide a renewed sense of hope.

o At Anglo American we are clear on our position: we are in the business of mining, not politics. The people of each country in which we operate choose their leaders according to their processes. We will work with those leaders and are interested in the policies that are adopted and how those policies are applied.

The people of each country in which we operate choose their leaders according to their processes. We will work with those leaders and are interested in the policies that are adopted and how those policies are applied.

To my Kaalvoet understanding, President Jacob Zuma was chosen as our leader, according to our processes, and yet, Anglo chose to disinvest. This Keynote address is tantamount to telling the voters of South Africa, to ensure that Anglo American's selected candidate / party are successful, if we wish their investment.

<u>*Let us repeat:*</u>

Had the mining industry, used only South African labour in their total labour force, and paid them maybe 60% of their 'own labour value', South Africa as a nation, would be wealthier today, both black and white, and the country, but the Rand Lords and the mining investors, would not have extracted the wealth that they did from us?

****

"Liberty, Equality, Fraternity"

The Political Constitution, that we have in South Africa today, in most parts of the world, originate from the French Revolution period, and the Declaration of the Rights of Man:

Declaration of the Rights of Man - 1789
Approved by the National Assembly of France, August 26, 1789

6.   **Law is the expression of the general will. Every citizen has a right to participate personally, or through his representative, in its foundation.** *It must be the same for all, whether it protects or punishes. All citizens, being equal in the eyes of the law, are equally eligible to all dignities and to all public positions and occupations, according to their abilities, and without distinction except that of their virtues and talents.*

1789, France brought us the basis, of what we know as our new western Political democracy, including the Declaration of the Rights of Man, resulting in France's famous constitutional maxim, **"Liberty, Equality, Fraternity"**.

According to 4th generation refugees, and the new flood of refugees, France appears to have failed on the

Fraternity pillar, most parts of the western world has, but possibly our better example is the Indian Constitution that is based on *"Liberty, Equality, Fraternity"*.

From an article that first appeared in The Conversation (theconversation.com) by Jeremie Gilbert a professor of international and comparative law, at the University of East London and David Keane, an associate professor in law, at Middlesex University, I extract the following:

The historical weight of the 1789 French revolution and its approach to citizenship cannot be underestimated in today's political and legal landscape. The "absolute" nature of equality is part of this legacy, with equality seen as the overarching principle in the constitutional edifice.

An outdated legal system

The French state's policy rejects any references to national, racial, ethnic, religious or linguistic minorities.

This model is based on the idea that the state should interact with the individual only, not communities or groups, in order to give equal treatment to everyone. "Absolute equality" is seen as the best way to ensure the integration of all citizens, to the benefit of both the state and the citizens themselves.

As a result, French authorities have rejected any form of targeted measures for ethnic, religious or linguistic groups. In practise this has rendered minorities invisible and brought systemic forms of discrimination.

I am of the opinion that there are many groups who believe they are 'invisible' in South Africa, we continue with "The Conversation'.

But we argue that another founding principle, that of fraternity, could be used to counterbalance the negative effects of this strict interpretation of the law regarding equality. Of the three terms in France's famous constitutional maxim, "Liberty, Equality, Fraternity", the legal significance of fraternity is the least understood.

From a legal perspective, its definition has always been problematic, and as our new research has highlighted, it is unquestionably the "weak link" in the trilogy.

But a more flexible interpretation of the term fraternity may make it possible to recognise minority rights within the French Republican model – without going against the existing bloc de constitutionnalité, which comprises all the fundamental constitutional values of the country. So far, the dominant focus on equality has meant a rejection of data collected on origin, race or religion.

Arguably, a focus on fraternity, which is also one of the fundamental constitutional values, could allow a much more flexible and encompassing approach to diversity within the country, and play an important role in diffusing the tensions that have been developing over the last few years.

'The Conversation' then introduces us to BR Ambedkar, involved in the Independence of India 1949 to 1950, and I trust that my support for BR Ambedkar will not be received as negatively as my support for Donald Trump's inaugural speech, when I expressed my desire for a South African leader, to say the same words that Trump had to say about being industry and jobs back to the people of the USA.

During a speech to the Constituent Assembly on November 25, 1949, Mr. BR Ambedkar gave the assembly three warnings, and we focus on the third, the most important of the three warning, in context of South Africa.

Excerpts from the speech to the Constituent Assembly on November 25, 1949

On 26th January 1950, India will be an independent country. What would happen to her independence? Will she maintain her independence or will she lose it again? This is the first thought that comes to my mind. It is not that India was never an independent country. The point is that she once lost the independence she had. Will she lose it a second time? It is this thought which makes me most anxious for the future.

The third thing we must do is not to be content with mere political democracy. We must make our political democracy a social democracy as well. Political democracy cannot last unless there lies at the base of it social democracy.

Social democracy

What does social democracy mean? It means a way of life which recognises liberty, equality and fraternity as the principles of life. These principles of liberty, equality and fraternity are not to be treated as separate items in a trinity. They form a union of trinity in the sense that to divorce one from the other is to defeat the very purpose of democracy.

Kaalvoet Comment:

Social Democracy, is what is missing in South Africa, and the Africanist who rejected the Freedom Charter in 1955, rejected it for this very reason.

Note the following paragraph:

Liberty cannot be divorced from equality, equality cannot be divorced from liberty. Nor can liberty and equality be divorced from fraternity. Without equality, liberty would produce the supremacy of the few over the many. Equality without liberty would kill individual initiative. Without fraternity, liberty would produce the supremacy of the few over the many. Without fraternity, liberty and equality could not become a natural course of things. It would require a constable to enforce them.

*We must begin by acknowledging the fact that there is complete absence of two things in Indian Society. One of these is equality. On the social plane, we have in India a society based on the principle of **graded inequality which we have a society in which there are some who have immense wealth as against many who live in abject poverty.***

*On the 26th of January 1950, we are going to enter into a life of contradictions. **In politics we will have equality and in social and economic life we will have inequality.** In politics we will be recognising the principle of one man one vote and one vote one value. In our social and economic life, we shall, by reason of* *our social and economic structure, continue to **deny the principle of one man one value.** How long shall we continue to live this life of contradictions? How long shall we continue to deny equality in our social and economic life? If we continue to deny it for long, we will do so only by putting our political democracy in peril. We must remove this contradiction at the earliest possible moment or else those who suffer from inequality will blow up the structure of political democracy which is Assembly has to laboriously built up.*

*The second thing we are wanting in is recognition of the principle of fraternity. What does fraternity mean? **Fraternity means a sense of common brotherhood of all** Indians — of Indians being one people. It is the principle which gives unity and solidarity to social life. It is a difficult thing to achieve. How difficult it is, can be realised from the story related by James Bryce in his volume on American Commonwealth about the United States of America.*

The story is — I propose to recount it in the words of Bryce himself:

"Some years ago the American Protestant Episcopal Church was occupied at its triennial Convention in revising its liturgy. It was thought desirable to introduce among the short sentence

prayers a prayer for the whole people, and an eminent New England divine proposed the words `O Lord, bless our nation'.

Accepted one afternoon, on the spur of the moment, the sentence was brought up next day for reconsideration, when so many objections were raised by the laity to the word nation' as importing too definite a recognition of national unity, that it was dropped, and instead there were adopted the words

`O Lord, bless these United States."

There was so little solidarity in the USA at the time when this incident occurred that the people of America did not think that they were a nation. If the people of the United States could not feel that they were a nation, how difficult it is for Indians to think that they are a nation?

A great delusion

I remember the days when politically minded Indians, resented the expression "the people of India". They preferred the expression "the Indian nation." **I am of opinion that in believing that we are a nation, we are cherishing a great delusion.** *How can people divided into several thousands of castes be a nation? The sooner we realise that we are not as yet a nation in the social and psychological sense of the world, the better for us. For then only we shall realise* *the necessity of becoming a nation and seriously think of ways and means of realising the goal. The realisation of this goal is going to be very difficult – far more difficult than it has been in the United States. The United States has no caste problem. In India there are castes. The castes are anti-national. In the first place because they bring about separation in social life. They are anti-national also because they generate jealousy and antipathy between caste and caste. But we must overcome all these difficulties if we wish to become a nation in reality. For fraternity can be a fact only when there is a nation. Without fraternity, equality and liberty will be no deeper than coats of paint.*

Kaalvoet Comment: South Africa's Rainbow nation, was no more that a few coats of paint, a nation is impossible without Fraternity, or as the Africanist will refer to it, 'The Brotherhood of Man'

These are my reflections about the tasks that lie ahead of us. They may not be very pleasant to some. But there can be no gainsaying that political power in this country has too long been the monopoly of a few and the many are only beasts of burden, but also beasts of prey. This monopoly has not merely deprived them of their chance of betterment, it has sapped them of what may be called the significance of life. These down-trodden classes are tired of being governed. They are impatient to govern themselves.

This urge for self-realisation in the down-trodden classes must not be allowed to devolve into a class struggle or class war. It would lead to a division of the House. That would indeed be a day of disaster. For, as has been well said by Abraham Lincoln, a House divided against itself cannot stand very long. Therefore the sooner room is made for the realisation of their aspiration, the better for the few, the better for the country, the better for the maintenance for its independence and the better for the continuance of its democratic structure. This can only be done by the establishment of equality and fraternity in all spheres of life. That is why I have laid so much stresses on them.

This speech was powerful, and it takes place at a time when the ANCYL, including Mandela, escalate the struggle for self-determination, from the 1943 ANC, Atlantic Charter Claim and Bill of Rights, to a new level with the ANC 1949 Programme of Action and Bill of Rights, Kaalvoet asks how the Charterists, and the SAIC, when exposed to the above speech, elected to sacrifice the black majority, by participating in the Freedom Charter anti-Africanist philosophy?

Selected Tribes

The Colonizer, as part of the process, selected tribes to assist them in the administration of the Colony, and securing their wealth interests. These selected tribes, caused further division in the Colony, and were given preference when the decolonization process takes place, resulting in the continued conflict that we have in Africa today.

The English in 1830, developed their first selected tribe, the Mfengu, and on May 14, 1835, introduced them to Africa, as the Mfengu, allegedly runaways from Shaka.

The Mfengu were 'emancipated' two days after Chief Hintsa was murdered, and Kaalvoet is of the opinion that Chief Hintsa, had become aware that the English, over a five years period, had developed their 'selected tribe', and that the selected tribe was now a military ally, and a threat to the freedom of the amaGcaleka and other clans.

The Mfengu, were not 'runaways' from Shaka, they were recruited from the amaGcaleka 'dogs of war', over a five year period, given land, taught to farm with cereal crops, and educated, before they were emancipated on May 14, 1835.

Of great importance to the context that Kaalvoet is presenting, is how, a 'tribe' was created by the English, between 1830 and 1835, and how easily, how successfully, these Nguni were educated, and skilled in manufacture and agriculture, and trained to be military allies of the English, and I ask, why did my white ancestors, not provide this development, for all Africans we interacted with?

The English would not have successfully defeated the Xhosa, the Zulu, or the Boer, without the investment in the Mfengu?

In *'Consider the Verdict'* the origins of the Mfengu, as related to me through the Kaalvoet spiritual world, is described as follows:

"Sirs, your history book reflect on the emancipation of the Mfengu by the English, as having collected all the homeless people, having run away from Shaka, finding themselves in the Eastern Cape, and drifting to Rev Ayliff in Butterworth."

"This is inaccurate. The majority of the Mfengu originate from our Ngwane clan, having left our home, following a clash with Dingswayo, when Shaka was still a young junior to him."

"My statement is as follows"

Shaka and his mother Nandi, were sheltered by Dingswayo, Shaka, once of age, became one of Dingswayo's Generals, only becoming Chief of his Zulu Clan in 1816.

The Mthethwa Clan included many smaller clans, and one of the sons, Godongwana, eager to take control of the Mthethwa, plotted to kill his father, the plot was uncovered, and Godongwana became a fugitive, somewhere around 1806.

Following the death of his father, Godongwana, having changed his name to Dingswayo, dethroned his brother, and became Chief of the Mthethwa.

During his travels, Dingswayo had become aware of the Delagowa Bay, as an outlet port for Ivory.

Determined to procure for himself some European goods, he encouraged his subjects to travel and trade. Consequently, a great development in crafts occurred. Milk dishes, pillows, ladles of cane and wood, and snuff spoons were all produced, and a kaross factory was established.

Competition for the hunting grounds and trade routes set the scene for conflict as the northern Nguni groups were increasingly drawn into ivory trading networks with the Portuguese at Delagoa Bay. From this time, the most powerful chiefs resorted to frequent grand-scale fighting.

We are part of the eastern Nguni group, mainly living on the eastern sea, from the Mzimkulu River in the South, to the Pongolo River in the North, living between the sea and the Mountain of Spears in the West.

As a seven year-old I was a junior warrior, needing to protect our cattle from other clans. Our wealth is measured by the cattle that we own, so as a herd-boy, I needed to protect our wealth.

I am proudly Ngwane, and my Chief was Chief Matiwane.

We did not run away from Shaka, in 1812, he was not Chief of the Zulu tribe, but a young general, subservient to Dingiswayo, King of the Mthethwa.

I was a very young boy, Dingswayo launched a campaign against us Ngwane who controlled the Nhlazatshe Mountain area. (Ulundi to Vryheid).

Dingiswayo was mobilising his forces, Shaka providing 1000, Dingiswayo 2500, and another 1000 from minor tribes, already part of the Zulu nation.

Our Chief Matiwane was a skilled military strategist, and a fearsome warrior. In order to survive, every group had their intelligence sources that would warn them of any attack. They would then decide whether they prepare to fight, or move out of danger, the fight or flight decision that every person and animal has.

Chief Matiwane was aware of the pending conflict and approached his neighbour, Chief Mtimkulu of the Hlubi tribe who arranged to hide our cattle in a safe hiding place. (Near Utrecht).

Chief Matiwane allowed our tribe to be forced into a quick surrender, our cattle safe and wishing to protect his people., and we were incorporated into the Mthethwa paramountcy.

Our culture permitted a victorious Chief to retain all cattle captured, plus the men, woman and children. The cattle and the captured people remained the possession of the victorious Chief, until some time that peace was made between the two conflicting groups, and then, a share of the cattle would be returned, and the captured people would be returned to their clan, subservient to the victorious Chief.

Soon after Matiwane's defeat, he approached Mtimkulu for permission to fetch our cattle, Mtimkulu refused to grant permission. The Ngwane forces attacked the Hlubi's killing many, including Mtimkulu, and recovering his cattle, and taking many Hlubi's captive with him.

Matiwane knew that this action would become known to Dingiswayo and Shaka, the Ngwane, only recently in battle, tired, and in possession of nearly 20 000 had of cattle, it would encourage Dingiswayo, to launch another attack, so he decided to move his people and his cattle towards the West to avoid another attack from Dingiswayo.

As a seven year-old I can remember our move from our homeland, having made the decision, Chief Matiwane set us into the West with the cattle, and he returned with a group of elders, and his main warriors, to move the rest of the clan.

As we moved west, we moved into conflict that is not unusual, we either negotiated grazing and water, or if need be, defended ourselves and our cattle.

As we moved west we faced aggressive resistance particularly from the Batlokwa tribe under Mantatisi, she was a tactician and powerful. She was in conflict with he own people as her son, the Chief, was still very young, and other family members were trying to unseat her. Under her, the Batlokwa was building though incorporating, small clans into her Batlokwa, and the area between Harrismith and Thab Nchu, was a hive of activity.

This Botlokwa clan, under Mantatisi was a large group, she was respected, always on the move, and the Ngwane kept their distance, and moved to settle under the Mountains of Spears.

Mantatisi move North West, 1823, heading into Botswana, and ran into an ambush, we heard that she then retreated, and settled in the Marabeng Mountains, where her son Sekonyela commanded the Tlokwa near the Caledon Valley.

Through to 1823, Sekonyela and Moshoeshoe competed for space, till Sekonyela succumbed, moving to Winburg, and allowing his people his group to be absorbed by Moshoeshoe, or move as small clans into the Orange Free State or the Cape Colony.

One morning, we had lived for almost a year in peace under the mountains near the Suthu, we were attacked by a mixed group of Dutch and Griquas on horseback. We were able to repel the attack, but not before the attackers were able to capture fifty of our front-line warriors. My brother Mavusu, was one of the captured.

That day we prepared for war, we would be ready to defend ourselves. Days passed, and nothing happened. The elders considered following those captured, but decided not to risk the group.

Two Khoikhoi arrived, messengers, negotiating with Chief Matiwane for his Hlubi captives, they wished to purchase them for the slave traders who had attacked us as few days earlier, as part of the transaction, they would return our brothers.

In our culture, any delegation who approaches another clan to negotiate, is guaranteed safe passage.

Chief Matiwane and the elders negotiated with the delegation all day, parading the Hlubi and Tlokwa captives as they negotiated compensation.

Our warriors sat on a nearby hill watching for any attack from the Slave Traders.

As the sun set, Chief Matiwane instructed his captives to kill the two negotiators, and before the sun rose the next morning, the Ngwane, under Matiwane retreated, moving east and south to where we eventually settled in 1823, north of the Umtata River, in a valley where we were protected from the north-west, from which the danger was expected, and to the south, across the river, were the amaPondo.

Six years after leaving our homeland, the Ngwane under Chief Matiwane had found a new home for his thirty-thousand followers and their 20 000 head of cattle.

Chief Matiwane soon became aware that many of the people, that were captured during local tribal conflicts, soon became the required supply that provided the needs of the slave traders in Delagoa Bay. This brought a few local Chiefs into the supply chain, where they found themselves part of the ivory trade, ivory and other goods, carried by the 'dogs of war', themselves, sold in Delagoa Bay.

Before the various tribes found their link to the ivory trade, their supply of slaves was limited, but once they entered the ivory trade, they exposed themselves, and their people, to the Portuguese traders, operating out of Delagoa Bay, rebel Griqua traders, English and Dutch groups.

During the battle of Mbolompo, we were defeated by the combined power of the English, with the Colonists, the Pondo, the Thembu and the amaGcaleka. We were captured, with our dogs of war, and all our cattle.

Sibongile, will tell you how us Ngwane were defeated during what they called the battle of Mbolompo in August 1928. She was taken by the English, Reverend Dee, women and children taken by the light-skins, us men distributed among the tribes.

A few years later, my sister Sibongile was used by Reverend Dee and the missionary to recruit five hundred Ngwane 'dogs of war', mainly from the amaGcaleka.

My father and two of my brothers were part of the recruits, and when I was fully trained, I helped Sibongile and Reverend Dee recruit and train what was to become the Mfengu military force.

All those who were trained were allocated land in the Kat River Valley, and while assisting the English in clashes with minor clans, we soon owned many cattle.

By 1834, when the recruits were fully trained as a military ally, we were encouraged into assisting the English to set up a war against the amaGcaleka. I was allocated a position near Chief Hintsa's Royal Kraal where I prepared the other 'dogs of war' to run away when the battle started, to take as many of the Gcaleka cattle as possible.

At this stage, we fully supported the war against the amaGcaleka, they were a threat to our new-found wealth, farms and cattle in the Kat River Valley.

We were then 'inspired' into setting up a meeting for the English with Chief Hintsa of the amaGcaleka.

Our family cooperated, never believing that Chief Hintsa would be asked to submit to the English, we knew he would not, but what followed, we never expected.

*****

By the time of their emancipation, 500 Mfengu had already been trained to ride horses, and were expert marksman, a military ally, that would support the English as they finally took the Eastern Cape, defeated the Zulu, and would be alongside the English, when they defeated the Boer.

The leaders of this 'selected tribe', as elders and masters of their tribal youth, would 'send' their young males to work on the mines, to bring income to the tribe, and wealth to their leaders.

Were they slaves, or were they just controlled?

Whichever, they became the profit base, for the mining industry.

The Mfengu, were very disappointed when they were moved out of the Kat River Valley, across the Kei River, by the English, integrating with the Thembu, but, the system only needed to empower a few financially, and the deed was done.

We use Nelson Mandela and the Long Walk to Freedom, to confirm the Kaalvoet opinion, we need to remember that in May 1835, when the Mfengu had been emancipated, they were allegedly no more than desperate Zulu's running away from Shaka, or so the 'fairy-tale' goes, it was impossible for the Shaka runaways, to achieve the status that is described by Nelson Mandela, if the English did not give the 'emancipated', intensive training and development.

Long Walk to Freedom

When I was a boy, amaMfengu were the most advanced section of the community and furnished our clergymen, policemen, teachers, clerks, and interpreters. They were also amongst the first to become Christians, to build better houses, and to use scientific methods of agriculture, and they were wealthier than their Xhosa compatriots. They confirmed the missionaries' axiom, that to be Christian was to be civilized, and to be civilized was to be Christian. There still existed some hostility toward amaMfengu, but in retrospect, I would attribute this more to jealousy than tribal animosity. This local form of tribalism that I observed as a boy was relatively harmless. At that stage, I did not witness nor even suspect the violent tribal rivalries that would subsequently be promoted by the white rulers of South Africa.

My father did not subscribe to local prejudice toward amaMfengu and befriended two amaMfengu brothers, George and Ben Mbekela. The brothers were an exception in Qunu: they were educated and Christian. George, the older of the two, was a retired teacher and Ben was a police sergeant.

If the reader can accept that the English Colonizer had selected and developed the Mfengu as their partner and Military ally, you will understand the Kaalvoet theory that the Afrikaner, in 1902, becomes the new selected tribe.

Mandela President Elect in 1955

Nelson Mandela becomes the newly elected Black South African President, elected by the Globalization Participants, as part of the 'Freedom Charter' in 1955. According to the Kaalvoet theory, he was identified as the suitable leader, through his association with the SACP and the SAIC in 1953, and the system would have transferred power to him and the ANC early 1960s, if the had majority support.

Kaalvoet's eyes were opened to the manipulation of the 'Freedom Charter' process, thanks to friend John Mahapa, one of the ANCYL, who were evicted from the ANC in 1958, he describes what occurred as follows:

"The Kliptown Charter, was written by the whites and the Indians, and they went to Kliptown, put us notices inviting the black people, to come and listen to the Charter, the blacks arrived, listened to these whites and Indians promising them freedom, and the all saluted them. The fools!!"

Off this comment, Kaalvoet researches until he finds a copy of *The AFRICANIST*, June / July 1958, Vol4 No,11, from which, we quote, and comment on the implications of the content.

<u>June / July 1958   The AFRICANIST,   VOL 4 NO 11   page 2b</u>

The Great Amalgamation:

In 1953 C.O.D. (Congress of Democrats) was born. Who her parents were and who the midwife was we unfortunately do not know. But rumour persists that she was the product of an incestuous Union. Be that as it may, she was born - at least we came to know of her existence, for the first time then.

In the same year rumours grew of an unholy alliance between the A.N.C. and this new body, and the SAIC. They were difficult to confirm, because no conference had adopted a resolution to that effect. The basis of co-operation was not defined. It has never been defined.

Kaalvoet Comment:
The Africanist appears to be making an allegation that the ANC, through Nelson Mandla, had an 'unholy alliance' with the C.O.D. and the SAIC, when no resolution had been passed by the ANC.

Queenstown Conference:

The first intimation the rank & file of Congress had of the shape of things to come, of the change in management, was the Queenstown Conference of 1953, when a former president, of the Youth League, Chief opponents in Congress, of the policy of Non-collaboration, led the assault on the *(1949)* Programme, unleashed by the Transvaal. the headquarters of the C.O.D.

The African people repulsed the attack on their programme vigorously and violently. The new management had begun to assert its authority.

Kaalvoet Comment:
The Africanist claims that the C.O.D., including a former president of the ANCYL. led the assault on the 1949 Programme, and that the African people repulsed the attack.

Durban Conference:

Nothing daunted by the reverses of the Queenstown Conference, the New Management again assailed the Programme at the Durban Conference, the following year, 1954. But this time it employed tactics which have come to be peculiarly its own distinctive tactics. It told Conference before hand, through its business journal, "New Age", what Conference would discuss and the lines that it "expected", (in the Directors Language) Conference to pursue. But in spite of brow-beating, the African people, defended the Programme. Again the Management was beaten.

****

Kaalvoet Comment:

The available documents relating to the ANC, annual 1954 Conference, gives no indication that the 1949 Programme was discussed, let alone objected to.

The ANC does pledge its support for the Call for 50 000 Freedom Volunteers, to assist the Congress of the People, in collecting information for the Charter.

Kaalvoet questions whether the document, researched, information collected, collated, in a time of restricted communication and travel, could warrant to be representative of all the people's wishes?

June / July 1958   The AFRICANIST, VOL 4 NO 11   page 2.c/3a

The Kliptown Charter.

Having realised that direct assault on the Programme of Action was doomed to failure, the management adopted another distinctive stunt. It produced the Kliptown Charter which is analysed on the pages of this bulletin.

We shall therefore, not comment on it.

The second half of 1955 was devoted to "Popularising the Charter" - the "popular" document which came form the "people". It had to be "popularised", never the less, - unlike the Programme which needed no "Popularisation". But the Charter failed to fire the imagination, not only of the African people, but of the New National group as well.

Bloemfontein Conference.

An attempt was made in December 1955 at the Bloemfontein Conference to impose the Charter on the people. Again, as in 1954 delegates to the conference read in C.O.D's business journal, "New Age" what the report of the National Executive of Congress would be. They read also that they were "expected" to "adopt" the Kliptown Charter. Conference was indignant at the impudence and insolence; and utter disregard for the dignity of the A.N.C. Conference displayed in the :New Age". First it should be remembered that the Durban Conference had seriously warned those responsible, that never again should "New Age" or any other paper, Act as the Custodians of the intelligence of the A.N.C. Conference. The bosses apparently had not been impressed.

It was decided by the Conference that the Kliptown Charter would be discussed at the Annual Conference in December, 1956. A Special Conference to consider the implementation of the Non-Collaboration aspect of the Programme, as well as the question of "Passes for Woman" was Conference to be held early in the new year.

Kaalvoet Comment:
The following published letter written by Walter Sisulu, in September 1955, must have been the precursor for the December 1955 Conference, and in September 1955, Walter Sisulu confirms that the 'drafting' of the Charter, has not reached the people.

Article in Fighting Talk by W.M. Sisulu: Forward with the Freedom Charter
26 September 1955

The Joint Executives of the four Congresses have correctly decided to campaign for the endorsement of the Charter by one million people from the multi-racial South African society. It seems clear that we cannot achieve this gigantic task of educating the people, popularising the Charter and obtaining one million signatures, without first examining the weaknesses which showed themselves during the C.O.P. campaign so that we can build on a foundation which is more solid after the experiences of that campaign. It is hardly necessary to enumerate all the weaknesses here. Suffice it to say that the organizational plan set up in the early stages of the C.O.P., the establishment of committees in every town, dorp, village or factory in the Union was not accomplished. We failed to link up the C.O.P. with our daily struggles. Many people in the movement, including some leaders in the ANC particularly, did not very well understand the C.O.P. They suspected it was to be a new organisation which would come to replace the ANC or to dominate the ANC. Some regarded the C.O.P. as nothing more than just a big conference unconnected with their positive struggles. Others thought it was an attempt by the leadership to evade the positive and militant struggle of the people against the Nationalist onslaught on their rights.

Kaalvoet Comment:
Walter Sisulu admits that the organization failed, "We failed to link up the C.O.P. with our daily

struggles, thus, logically, the Freedom Charter does not represent the peoples wishes, ANC leadership avoiding the militant struggle of the people.

Article in Fighting Talk by W.M. Sisulu: Forward with the Freedom Charter
26 September 1955

The People's Era

Once our people understand the Charter and its significance, the attainment of economic and political power in our lifetime nothing can stand in the way of making its demands a reality.

The opening of the campaign for one million signatures has begun; yet the important thing about the campaign for the Freedom Charter is not just the collection of signatures; nor is it just the bringing of the ideas of the Charter to every home and making them the golden household words of the people.

This is, by itself, very good indeed, but the important thing is that the overwhelming majority of the South African population should proclaim the "Freedom Charter" as their guiding star. In other words, they must understand fully the meaning, the inspiration and the significance of the Charter. As someone has already said the end of the C.O.P. was but a beginning. The campaign which produced the "Freedom Charter" was the beginning of our great campaign, of the building from our multi-racial society of a united nation, free from poverty and misery, free from racial strife and antagonism. It is our hardest campaign which will bring to the broad masses of our people the understanding that they have much more in common than the things which superficially appear to divide them; that they have nothing to lose but much to gain, from the victory of the "Freedom Charter".

The government have great fear of the "Freedom Charter". They know how powerful the "Freedom Charter" movement can be, and how it can fire the imagination of the millions of our people. They are haunted by the knowledge that the Charter means the beginning of the end of their era and the opening of a new era the People's Era of Freedom!

This launch of the one million signature campaign, to give credence to the document they call the 'Freedom

Charter' seems to have died at the 1955 December Conference?

****

Media and archive material will link Professor ZK Matthews and Bernstein to having jointly drafted the 'Freedom Charter', yet, Matthews, in his address at the 1955 annual ANC Conference, he makes the following comment;

A most important aspect of the Congress was the adoption of the Freedom Charter. That document is going to be placed before this Conference in the course of your deliberations.
*I shall therefore not say anything about it at this stage except to remind you that the Freedom Charter was drawn up, not by the African National Congress but by the Congress of the People and it is therefore necessary for you **to ratify** the Freedom Charter and to make it part, **if you so desire,** of the policy of the African National Congress.*

Most Veteran ANC stalwarts, talk highly about Dr. A.B. Xuma, his leadership and what he did for the ANC. I present extracts for his letter written to the ANC President-General and Delegates to the Annual 1955 Conference of the ANC;

18 December 1955
The President-General and Delegates to the Annual Conference
of the African National Congress.
Fellow Africans,

I send you, one and all, heartiest greetings. My apologies and regrets for inability to attend this important Annual Conference.

In following up the affairs of the African National Congress one is alarmed as well as distressed over certain tendencies which have developed in Congress in recent years.

These tendencies are undermining and weakening the Congress as a National Liberation Movement and mouthpiece of the African people. To mention but a few I would say:

1. *The African National Congress has lost its identity as a National Liberation Movement with a policy of its own and distinct African Leadership. One hears or reads of statements by the "Congresses" and one hardly ever gets the standpoint of the African National Congress. As such, many Africans are confused and wonder who are their leaders and whom must they follow as a consequence.*
2. *The National Movement is disintegrating into splinters of disaffected groups, such as the ANC (National-Minded Block) and the Bantu National Congress, besides the African National Congress. This causes much confusion in the loyalty of the Africans.*
   We cannot ignore these divisions whatever their respective strength. Their very existence weakens and undermines and brings mockery to our National struggle as a National aspiration of our people.

Then I remind you that when I took over leadership of the Congress in 1940 the Transvaal was divided into seven sections, Natal into two and the Cape Province into two and the Orange Free State could only claim Bloemfontein for the Congress.

Now you can see why my heart bleeds when I see the emergence of these splits, cracks, antagonisms and struggle for office for personal reasons and control of the Organisation which we had healed and buried after I took over the leadership. There were none in 1949.

3. *The National Congress seems to fear to face criticisms constructive and otherwise from it's following and others. People who voice their reasonable and considered views on Congress policy and/or no policy and on actions in the name of the African National Congress are referred to as "sellers-out" or "agents" or "friends of the Government" instead of being shown where they are wrong.*

   Many who dare to criticise the hierarchy have been expelled or "liquidated" individually or en masse without a democratic hearing.

   This attitude is foreign to Congress as a democratic movement and smacks of totalitarianism or authoritarianism which a movement like Congress cannot countenance and still claim to be fighting for freedom from domination and suppression.

4. ***The Congress leadership seems to have turned their backs against the African National Congress Nation-building Programme of the 1940s and have even forgotten the Congress Charter of Human Rights "The Africans` Claims" in South Africa of December 16, 1945, which can only be superseded by the Charter of Human Rights of the United***

Nations instead of other vague, inconclusive so-called charters, which merely defer and confuse the Africans` just and immediate claims.

Congress agreed in 1946 to co-operate with other non-European fellow-nationals on all points of common interest but insisted that the respective national organisations must maintain their identity as integrated regiments in the struggle for common citizenship.

This was intended to make each organisation play its full part in the struggle and bear the necessary sacrifices. It was to avoid the danger of sections using others without making sacrifices themselves.

Many of the delegates are new in Congress. To them I say: Ask the old stalwarts with whom I have struggled in the forties where we stood then.

Above all, ask my " Kindergarten Boys" of the African National Congress Youth League whose foundation representatives met with me in my library at home and were baptised and established by me and the late Mr. R. V. Selope Thema at the BMSC in Johannesburg as the African National Congress Youth League, what they stood for. To them I say remember the 1940s, Remember Africa!

5. *By acting on the principle "of action for action`s sake and for propaganda reasons" instead of aiming at achieving results, Congress, through the Defiance Campaign, the Western Areas Removal Scheme and the School Boycott, the Congress aroused vain hopes in the breasts of the struggling Africans and made promises of "secret weapons" and "provision of services" for which no preparations were made.*

It will be wise for Congress not to embark on revolutionary tactics unless the leaders with the rank are prepared to pay the price.

If leaders arouse the masses and the leaders then fail the masses in the testing hour the loyalty and faith of the masses is shaken in the leadership, and what is worse, in the Organisation itself.

Such actions, under the circumstances, tended to set the clock of our progress back many years.

I appeal to the Annual Conference to rescind its resolution of School Boycott.

With no effective alternative system of education, the boycott of schools with its interference with children and teachers, is bound to be worse for African progress than Bantu Education; in fact, it is not only negative but harmful in that in the long run, it will cause the African people to turn against the ANC.

I must appeal to all delegates to make this Conference one of the most constructive conferences, for examination and re-assessment of our methods, policies and attitudes.

One and all must realise no one else will ever free the Africans but the Africans themselves.

Their genuine friends can help them, but the Africans themselves must rely on themselves.

We must learn to do things for ourselves in order to grow, to plan our programme and campaigns and rely upon our own leadership.

Until we can do that, have faith in ourselves as well as self-reliance, depend upon our inner strength, we do not deserve freedom and could not maintain it if it were offered us on a platter.

Let us re-organise our people, re-integrate the African National Congress as the mouthpiece of the African people.

We must organise ourselves not against other nationals, or to gain anything at anyone else's expense, but only that we must gain strength in our unity because "charity begins at home" and there can be no internationalism without nationalism.

Leadership means service for and not domination over others.

True and genuine leaders serve the cause of the people and do not expect the cause to serve them or become a source of profit and honour for them.

Africa expects all her sons and daughters to serve the cause of the people loyally, sincerely and honestly.

Let us close ranks, fellow-Africans and do our duty.

I wish your deliberations every success.

"Right not might, freedom not serfdom."

Yours for the cause,

A B Xuma

Kaalvoet Comment:

When I read Dr. A B Xuma's letter dated December 18, 1955, my negative attitude towards the Freedom Charter grows, and, with Nelson Mandela's criticism of AB Xuma, in the Long Walk to Freedom, I surprisingly, do not find this letter challenged in Congress.

<u>*The Kliptown Charter;*</u>

<u>*Kaalvoet Comment:*</u>

The content that follows is the Africanist analysis of the Kliptown Charter, or more commonly known in ANC circles, as the Freedom Charter, ending with the Africanist Rejection of the Charter.

In legal parlance, silence on the matter, is acceptance, I think?

This document is dated June/July 1958, months before the Africanists were forcibly evicted form the ANC.
I believe that every South African is entitled to the written response that would be part of this democracy that the 'Freedom Charter' represents, my challenge to the Charterists, is to provide a response to this REJECTION, that would remove any substance, to my allegation that the Freedom Charter extended the length of Apartheid by 34 years, because of the failure to maintain the united ANC and their 1949 Programme of Action;
In the Africanist Magazine reproduction below, I present the extract in italics and in bold or underlining where attention and answers are required.

****

Rejection of the Charter. (The summary statement):

We reject the Kliptown Charter. We reject it as a document super-imposed on us. We reject it as a quasi-nationalist document with its attempt to laud the struggle for independence 'of all the peoples of South Africa' while undermining that struggle in the Southern tip of the land; **with its attempt to super impose ethnic grouping upon the future development of South Africa and thus make a mockery of the brotherhood of man, and man's common humanity.** We reject it as a pseudo-democratic document wishing to super impose a false brand of democracy which attempts to ignore the grim brand of realities of the Situation.

Above all, we reject it for its utter contempt of the African's mind and its ability and capacity to grapple with the Social question the problem of man's relation to his fellowman. **Such behaviour is a slur on the African's intellect and an insult to his intelligence.**

Dear Liberal;

May I extend an invitation to you, to submit your reasons for why the Africanist, was wrong, to reject the Freedom Charter?

Kaalvoet de la Harpe cedric@cedricdelaharpe.co.za

June / July 1958   The AFRICANIST,   VOL 4 NO 11   page 15a.

The Kliptown Charter.

By Ufford Khoruba and Kwame Lekwame

The expulsion of messes. Potlako Leballo and Josiah Madsunya, form the ANC, on the grounds of inter alia, of their rejecting the so called Freedom Charter and actively and consistently opposing it, precipitates a critical objective study of the document. Since we reject charterism and embrace Africanism, it behoves us to understand what we reject as thoroughly as what we accept.

Policy Statement:

It is a popular maxim of Western legalists that the preamble to any law is not in itself law but is deeper in significance than the law: since it, in that sense, gives the real intentions of the legislature. The Charter is not a statute but is a political document, and as such its opening clause must be taken to be of deeper significance than the provisions of its actual text. Its preamble contains basic notions and guiding ideas all leading to the fundamental principles within whose framework its details are adumbrated. What over the effects of a superficial study of its basic ideas that clearly reveals to us the real intentions of its authors.

The charterists claim that their charter is the policy of the A.N.C. as 'policy outlines basic principles'. According to informed opinion policy is a system of measured regulating the affairs of any body. It is, therefore clear that policy measures are intended to advance the organisation towards the attainment of its goals which are founded upon basic principles.

To have any realism at all such principles must be related to the actual material conditions. That much cannot be said for the ill-digested ideas and ill-defined statements catalogued in the ill-starred document the Kliptown Charter. One thing is certain; whatever the charter is, it is not a statement of policy.

<u>Kaalvoet Comment:</u>

I am of the opinion that the Freedom Charter was only ratified by the ANC in November 1958?

****

<u>The Authors of the Kliptown Charter.</u>

We are in a position to determine the authorship of the charter form analysis of the real nature and role of the leadership associated with its conception, pre-natal growth, its birth and ill-fated existence.

Professor Z.K. Matthews, Vice President of the A.N.C., moved the resolution that led to the birth of the Kliptown

Charter. As soon as the charter was born, the professor unequivocally disowned its authorship.

Opening with the words, "We, the people of South Africa declare for all our country and the world to know", the charter proceeds to list, its leading ideas in five consecutive clauses.

The phrase "We the people of South Africa" falsifies history and negates the realism of the situation. It is clear that the Charter is not a representative document. It does not represent the interest of the oppressed people of South Africa, but those of the oppressing aliens in it.

The Kliptown Charter did not emanate as a finished document form the A.N.C. It emanated as such form the Vodka Cocktail parties of Parktown and Lower Houghton. A close study of its ideas shows clearly that it bears the imprint of its origin. The black masses who met at Kliptown were merely pawns in the game of power politics.

The whites who were at Kliptown, except the special branch, were mainly members of the Congress of the Democrats. They are part of the ruling class in South Africa. While ostensibly fighting for the "progressive" South Africa, they are in reality concerned with the maintenance of the status quo.

The material position of members of the South African Indian Congress who were present, is identical with that of the members of the C.O.D. **These elements were the Indian Merchant Class who though politically repressed are in fact**

not oppressed. They are an exploiting alien groups whose material interests are in direct conflict with those of the Indian masses.

The African leaders present were mainly elements receiving economic benefits form the 'Marshall Aid Plan' of the C.O.D & SAIC.

To claim, therefore, that the Kliptown Charter was the work of independent, free and representative agents of either the Europeans, Indian, Coloured or African people, is to make a claim unsupported by facts.

The Basic Conception Underlying Ownership.

The statement of the first clause the "South Africa belongs to all who live in it" is incorrect. It is equivalent to saying that japan belongs to all people who live in it, yellow and white - all because the American Army occupation is resident in Japan. Such declaration would shock all Japan and all the world. South Africa is a part of Africa and even inch of Africa belongs to the Africans. The basic conception underlying ownership involves physical control and it is, therefore, a fundamental right of the African people to control their country.

The statement that no government can justly claim authority unless it is based on the will of all the people is tautological nonsense. The national government of any country must be based on the will of its nationals, excluding its non-nationals. In making the claim on the basis of just authority the CODDITES (sic) are clearly outdemocrating themselves - for even in a democracy just authority is based on the will of the majority. The statement is intellectually dishonest though politically expedient.

<u>Robbers and the Robbed.</u>

The second clause of the preamble states, "We the people … declare … that our people have been robbed of their birth right to land liberty and peace by a form of government founded on injustice and inequality." The "people's people" have been robbed, by the people? No. By an abstraction. By a form of government. No more classic examples can be found to illustrate the confusion of thought in which the charterists have landed themselves, and the slip of the pen of which they are just victims. Their political chicanery has landed them in a muddy muddle.

The truth is that the African people have been robbed by the European people. The use of the term 'land' is intentionally legerdemain . It is used to mean 'real estate' and reflect country through association. The deeper truth is that we have been robbed of our birthright to the effective control or our own country, and consequently, of our freedom, independence and happiness.

With the C.O.D. anxious as it is to confer on us the benevolence of their political despotism they must perforce refer to land in its agrarian sense, and not in the sense of its wider implications. They cannot, therefore, interpret it as a very source of our sustenance and maintenance.

The use of the word 'liberty' which implies a limited type of freedom is also significant as the word 'freedom' itself appears by design in the title only and nowhere in the actual text of the charter. The C.O.D. has no intention of conferring

freedom, independence and happiness on the African people, but only 'land liberty and peace'.

The charter complains about a form of government founded on injustice and inequality imply a general acceptance of the existing framework C.O.D. fails to appreciate that the existing form of government is based on oppression and degradation.

These social phenomena spell a greater degree of social maladjustment than injustice and inequality.

When in Rome.

Our country will never be prosperous or free until all our people live in brotherhood, enjoying equal rights and opportunities.

The final stamp of the genius of the social order or any social philosophy that purports to solve he social problem must be found in its evaluation of the relation of man to his fellowman, or what social thinkers and writers throughout the ages have called the 'brotherhood of man'.

Recognising as we do, the non-existence of inescapable differences between various branches or sub-branches of the human family and recognising also that whatever differences there are among various groups are especially due to environmental influences, we must regard any social unit based on ethnic grouping as a denial of the common community of men.

Much of Christ's disciples and followers have let him down on the practice of human brotherhood, his precepts remain classic: Love your neighbour as yourself, do unto others what you would be done to you, and finally his conception of a society in which they would be neither Jew nor Gentile. The freedom charter accepts as basic for the South African Social set up the continued existence of ethnic or national groups. It fails to realise that the existence of a European national group, or an Asia one in Africa is a serious anomaly, a contradiction in terms. The logically correct place to develop, as the charter postulates, Indian folklore and Indian customs is India and for Europeans to foster European folklore, and European Culture, is Europe. It is impossible for people who, out of arrogance born of their 'ethnic origins' or in the more grandiloquent phraseology of the charter, out of their 'race or national pride', describe their hosts, in terms of themselves as Non-European, non-white to grasp the real meaning and significance of brotherhood.

Be that as it may, the African people cannot accept the theory or practice of an outlook super-imposed upon them by elements whose guiding maxim seems to be; "When you are in Rome do as you so at home"?

C.O.D. Type of Democracy

"Only a democratic State, based on the will of all the people can secure to all their birthright without distinction of race, colour, sex or belief."

All forms of government are the machinery for the upholding of economic interests. In the struggle such as ours, the objective is to control such machinery. Such a government will obviously derive its just authority form the will of the African people. What the charterists fail to appreciate is that no writ of prescription can run against the fundamental rights of the African people, and certainly no such writ can run against the fundamental right of the African people to control effectively the source of their sustenance and maintenance.

With indecent haste the charterists declare that "the people shall share the country's wealth'. It is theoretically untenable and therefore politically unacceptable to have the robber and his victim to agree to share before the victim has vindicated his right of possession. It is, therefore as clear as day light, that the African cannot accept this C.O.D. type for democracy.

Equality of Master and Slave.

"And therefore, we the people of South Africa" concludes the preamble. "black and white together, — equals, country men and brothers, - adopt this Freedom Charter. And we pledge ourselves to strive together, sparing nothing of our strength and courage, until the democratic changes here set our, have been one."

The charterists are very unrealistic. The actual existing material conditions and the prevailing ideological divide have no meaning for them. The reconciliation between an out-groups and an in-group on both the material and

<u>intellectual levels before the synthesis of opposites can be real has no meaning for them. To them master and slave, — the exploiter and the exploited, the oppressor and the oppressed, the degrader and the degraded, are all EQUALS, TO THEM African Nationals and alien Nationals, — the dispossessed indigenous peoples and their alien dispossessors are all COUNTRY MEN. For them the tribalist and the nationalist, the Herrenvolkenist and the Africanist are all BROTHERS.</u>

The Problem of the synthesis of opposites cannot be resolved by a magic wand. It is dependent for its resolution upon changes in the material set-up, changes in the ideological content and changes in philosophic outlook to end the relationship of master and slave exploitation must be eliminated. **For the alien nationals to become African nationals they must restore the control of the country to the Africans and be nationalised by them.**

For the tribalist to become nationalist he must stop thinking in terms of ethnic or national groups in the country and think in terms of one social group the African nation. **<u>For the Herrenvolkenist to become an Africanist he must think in terms of the primacy of the interests of the subject class instead of that of those of the ruling class</u> the only basis for reconciliation of these interests.**

It is only after these stages, of social development have been gone through that we shall reach those categories of EQUALS, COUNTRY MEN AND BROTHERS — which betray no instability.

June / July 1958   The AFRICANIST,   VOL 4 NO 11   page 18a.

The text of the Charter.

Having dealt with the underlying notions of the guiding ideas which lead to the fundamental principles of the Charter we shall now deal with some of the salient points of its text.

Methods of upholding the Interests of the African people.

The Charter promises Votes for all, participation in the administration of councils of State at different levels. Here it is important to distinguish the mere democratic methods and procedures form democracy as a fundamental principle. In spite of their lip service to the methods and procedure of democracy, the Charterists understand these to mean in practice the carrying out of "directives" form higher organs by the masses — the towing of the line   by them. For them, the top leadership is the brains trust of the masses. When therefore, they mouth slogans such as THE PEOPLE SHALL GOVERN, these must mean, as long as it suits the top leaders and their lackeys and flunkies.

Political democracy has been defined old Abe Lincoln "as the government of the people for the people by the people." It means Government of the people by the freely elected representative of the majority, and in the interests of that majority as to what their real interests are.

We have observed that the function of all government is the upholding of economic interests. The crucial question about any form of government, therefore is:- Whose economic interest does it uphold? Since in South Africa the social question is primary a national question, any form of government in this country must uphold the economic interests of the African people. It is this fundamental principle that the Kliptown Charter fails to appreciate. Within the framework of acceptance of this fact, political democracy must be understood to comprise the methods and procedures whereby the African majority shall uphold their own economic interests. Questions of suffrage, election, participation in governmental and administrative organs of the state, are all properly within the purview and scope of political democracy. Properly conceived it is an outflow of Social democracy.

The Organisational Principle for Upholding the Interests of the African People

Democracy as a fundamental organisational principle is, therefore, the control by the majority of the machinery for upholding its economic interests. In South Africa it implies control exercised by the African majority. The function of social democracy is to control economic interests, to organise and plan economic activities and to distribute, on an equitable basis, national wealth. We have already alluded to the C.O.D. type of social democracy. In visualising, inter alia, the continual existence of domestic and the abolition of only 'fenced locations' the Charter bears the imprint of its origin. In passing it may be pointed out that in omitting the right of the workers to strike before social democracy is attained, the charterists successfully refute their own allegation that the Charter is a statement of policy.

Charity Begins at Home:

We owe no apology to the Charterists and we offer none in stating the inherent right of the indigenous people to control the machinery for the upholding of their own interests to be the fundamental of human rights.

If the Charterists accept, as we hope they do, one of the fundamental aims of education as pronounced by the United Nations, they will, to borrow their own phraseology, 'Pledge themselves to strive together, sparing nothing of their strength and courage, to foster respect for this fundamental right.

On the basis of the foregoing we conceive of a new nation in South Africa, a social unit, occupying a compact territory, sharing common social institutions. When the charter says "The right of all the peoples of Africa to independence and self government shall be recognised" we are tempted to remind them that 'charity begins at home'.

Kaalvoet must repeat:

Rejection of the Charter.

We reject the Kliptown Charter. We reject it as a document super-imposed on us. We reject it as a quasi-nationalist document with its attempt to laud the struggle for independence 'of all the peoples of South Africa' while undermining that struggle in the Southern tip of the land; with its attempt to super impose ethnic grouping upon the future development of South Africa and thus make a mockery of the brotherhood of man, and man's common humanity. We reject it as a pseudo-democratic document wishing to super impose a false brand of democracy which attempts to ignore the grim brand of realities of the Situation.

Above all, we reject it for its utter contempt of the African's mind and its ability and capacity to grapple with the Social question the problem of man's relation to his fellowman. Such behaviour is a slur on the African's intellect and an insult to his intelligence.

****

Kaalvoet Comment:

Supporters of the Charterists, the Freedom Charter, will be calling for me to retract my criticism of what we, the economic community, see as the success of the Freedom Charter, and the Charterists contribution to the freedom of the African people.

May I use the words of Messrs. Khoruba and Lekwame, under the heading of 'The Common Good', where they so eloquently call for the Charterists to provide an understanding of their 'inner compulsions' that propelled them:-

<u>The Common Good.</u>

<u>Perhaps if we understand thoroughly the inner compulsions propelling the authors of the Charter we may decide 'not to weigh their merits but to pardon their offences'.</u> The first of these influences is the instinctive tendency of every ruling class to uphold its economic interests as long as it possibly can. the second is the 'missionary zeal' of the apostles of a new found ideology, who believing as they do in the inherent superiority of their brand of ideology over all others, whether that ideology be theoretically valid or not, feel themselves compelled to spread their gospel and recreate the subject peoples in their own image, regardless of the chance of success.

In justice to the Charterists it must be pointed out that their contempt for the African and their utter disregard of his feelings are not for him, as such, but are a contempt and a disregard for the human personality.

This attitude flows from their philosophical position which regards man as an economic animal instead of a social being. Judged by the standards of the United Nations' Charter, our Kliptown Charterists, are barbarous and uneducated.

According to the United Nations Charterists, one of the fundamental aims of education is to develop the Human personality. Since the Kliptown charterists, unlike their United Nations counterpart, observe conspiratorial silence on the point, and since some of them are familiar with the maxim: "form each according to his capacity to each according to his needs", we may be allowed to quote them as a parting gift, the words of one wise old writer on the subject: "Men are not equal in their capacity to serve the Community nor are they equal in their needs but they are equal in the possession of a personality that is worthy of reverence. They are equal in the right to the development of that personality, so far as may be compatible with the common good. And in determination of what constitutes that common good they have an equal claim that their case should be heard and weighed, and that the judgement should be disinterest and just".

****

<u>Annual Conference.</u>

In 1957, the Annual Conference was held at the Communal Hall, Orlando. It had now become obvious that the Kliptown Charter could not chart the road to freedom. A diversion was necessary. Tho Programme of Action was again attacked. Again, the African masses, most of them blind followers of the present leadership defended their programme.

<u>Attack on Africanists.</u>

Attack on Africanists, the core around whom opposition to the Management was crystallising, became a regular feature of "New Age", C.O.D. business journal as well of its sister propaganda sheets, "Liberation" and "Fighting Talk". The more the bankruptcy of the A.N.C. leadership was exposed, the more regular the more violent and the harsher the attacks on the Africanist became.

Then came the 'Stay-at-Home' flop. We need not and will not comment on that, except to point out that it showed a new mood in the management.It showed that C.O.D. having come to realise that her authority, though established over the leadership. is being consistently repudiated by the African people had decided to destroy what she could not control.

She is now hell-bent on discrediting the A.N.C. and finally destroying it.

Kaalvoet Comment:
Mandela admits to having a changed philosophy from his 1949 position, Nelson Mandela admits to selling out his Africanist brothers, the sell-out allegations, are confirmed in his own words.

<u>*Long Walk to Freedom*</u>
Some in the ANC, particularly the Africanist contingent, who were anti-Communist and antiwhite, objected to the

charter as being a design for a radically different South Africa from the one the ANC had called for throughout its history. They claimed the charter favored a socialist order and believed the COD and white Communists had had a disproportionate influence on its ideology. In June 1956, in the monthly journal Liberation, I pointed out that the charter endorsed private enterprise and would allow capitalism to flourish among Africans for the first time. The charter guaranteed that when freedom came, Africans would have the opportunity to own their own businesses in their own names, to own their own houses and property, in short, to prosper as capitalists and entrepreneurs.

Not many years before, Nelson Mandela was 'anti-white', and my question to all the whites, both conservative and liberal, is their any reason for a black person not to have anti-white feelings?

It should be the basis off which the black youth enter adult-hood, and society should find 'common cause', a 'common bond', which will allow any anti-white to fade.

<u>The Expulsions:</u>
The expulsions of Madzunya and Leballo runs true to pattern. Those in Cape Town, as well as those in

Johannesburg who get "new Age" by air mail, read on Tuesday May 22, that those two congressites had been expelled.   The letter was signed by Duma Nokwe, who styles himself "Assistant Secretary General".

The actual letter of expulsion, signed by Mr. Duma Nokwe "Assistant Secretary General" was delivered to Mr. Leballo, on Thursday night 22nd May, 1958. It was dated the 22nd May. In other words the world knew that these Congrossites had been expelled, before they themselves knew. Their branches we learn, have not yet been informed of the expulsion or those branch officials.

Those are facts. There is only one conclusion to be drawn form them, namely that C.O.D. controls and dominated the A.N.C.. Leballos's and Madzunya's crime is that they refuse to submit to that domination.

We therefore call on the African people to condemn and reject all C.O.D. domination NOW. Otherwise the organisation we have built over the years, the programme we have created and the struggles we have so gloriously fought, will be reduced to ashes,

We declare, here and now, that we shall never submit to C.O.D. domination nor shall we ever permit C.O.D. to destroy what the African people have laboured so hard to create.

MAYIBUYE!!!!!!!!

****

November 1, 1958, the final nail:

From*: LION OF AZANIA: THE STORY OF ZEPHANIA LEKOAME*
   MOTHOPENG (1913 to 1990).
   (Master of Arts Thesis submitted to the University of Witwatersrand)   by Ali Hlongwane

Tension between the Charterists and Africanists reached boiling point at a conference held on November 1 and 2, 1958. Alert Luthuli, President of the ANC, spoke at the conference. He wasted no time in raising the alarm at what he referred to as 'white pandering to racialism' by the Nationalist Party. This tendency, in his view, led some in the ranks of the oppressed to 'emulate the nationalists in claiming exclusive control of South Africa. We have seen developing—even though in its embryonic stage—a dangerously narrow African Nationalism'.

These remarks, clearly directed at the Africanists in the conference, provoked a fierce debate. Can Themba, who was writing for Drum magazine at the time, reported:

'Mr. Z. Mothopeng is the first speaker. He says that he does not care about a multi-racial society. In this country the people are divided into two groups only: the oppressor and the oppressed. There can be no cooperation with oppressors.'

From: *LION OF AZANIA: THE STORY OF ZEPHANIA LEKOAME MOTHOPENG (1913 to 1990).*

(Master of Arts Thesis submitted to the University of Witwatersrand)   by Ali Hlongwane

Later, a dispute arose around credentials. Most of the branches with Africanist leanings were disqualified. ANC volunteers 'openly wielding sticks, clubs, and sjamboks' ensured that the targeted faction cold not enter the hall and be part of the conference. The Africanists held a caucus outside the hall. They resolved that the time had come for the parting of ways. This was related to the conference in a letter signed by Selby Ngendane, which in part read:

'It has, however, come to our notice that armed thugs have been brought in great numbers, at the invitation of the present ANC leadership for the specific purpose of murdering certain Africanists who are regarded as leading persons in the movement. Ours, Mr. Speaker, is a political battle aimed against the oppressor. We are not a para-military clique, engaged in the murder of fellow Africans … We are launching out openly, on our own, as the custodians of the ANC policy as it was formulated in 1912 and pursued up to the time of the Congress Alliance.'

Rossette Nziba was chosen to be the emissary of the Africanist message to the congress. However, he was unable to deliver the document as he was sent flying out of the conference hall.

And so, the Africanists forcibly evicted by the Congress management, declare themselves the custodians of the ANC policy, formulated in 1912, and improved on in 1949.

History will define our protagonist Robert Sobukwe, as having packed his bags and left like a small boy, objecting to the fathers attitude.

*****

On February 3, 1960, British Prime Minister Harold Macmillan warns of African National Consciousness, while congratulating the South African Parliament, for being destined to free the 'first of the Africanist Nationals;

Extract from Prime Minister, Harold Macmillan speech in South African Parliament February 3, 1960.

In the twentieth century, and especially since the end of the war, the processes which gave birth to the nation states of Europe have been repeated all over the world. We have seen the awakening of national consciousness in peoples who have for centuries lived in dependence upon some other power. Fifteen years ago this movement spread through Asia. Many countries there, of different races and civilisations, pressed their claim to an independent national life.

*Today the same thing is happening in Africa, and the most striking of all the impressions I have formed since I left London a month ago is of the **strength of this African national consciousness.** In different places it takes different forms, but it is happening everywhere.*

The wind of change is blowing through this continent, and whether we like it or not, this growth of national consciousness is a political fact. We must all accept it as a fact, and our national policies must take account of it.

Well you understand this better than anyone, you are sprung from Europe, the home of nationalism, here in Africa you have yourselves created a free nation. A new nation. Indeed in the history of our times yours will be recorded as the first of the African Nationalists.

****

Kaalvoet analysis of this comment:

At this stage of proceedings, the English, the wealth of the world, was about to release Nelson Mandela as the first African Nationalist President, just did not know that he did not have the support of the African.

****

<u>Boy Scout - 'Bob a Job' to Freedom Fighter</u>

John Mahapa, arrested with Robert Sobukwe on March 21, 1960, has greatly contributed towards my Africanist mindset development, born in 1940, still a child in 1955, my friend that moved form Boy Scout to Freedom Fighter overnight, thanks to the Drum Magazine.

To my surprise, many young Township boys belonged to Scout Groups in the Townships. Twice a year, during their school holidays, they were required to perform 'Bob a Job' doing work in their communities, earning a 'Bob', which was added to their Scout Troop coffers.

While still a student at an Orlando East Primary School, one of the community leaders, Job Rathebe, offered the Boy Scouts an opportunity to earn money for themselves. Friday afternoons, Saturdays, and on occasions Sunday mornings, they worked at the Drum Magazine, rolling and packing Drum magazines for distribution.

Early struggle by the South African black people, was driven by the educated groups, the Fort Hare students, the academics, the lawyers, the teachers, the journalists, the doctors, who brought together their friends and families as momentum built.

The Orlando East Secondary School youth, were bubbling with energy as they awakened to the Freedom movements in other parts of Africa, form living in a situation where freedom was not thought about, freedom not considered, almost impossible, they were becoming enlightened, they were the youth that ignited the fight for freedom, a fight that has been hidden form our heritage.

The Drum magazine, reading while rolling, while packing, brought them exposure to the African countries fight for freedom, the youth moved towards achieving dignity and freedom;

Jomo Kenyatta:
The "dangerous explosion" among the Kikuyu that he had predicted in 1930 erupted as the Mau Mau rebellion of 1952, which was directed against the presence of European settlers in Kenya and their ownership of land. On October 21, 1952, Kenyatta was arrested on charges of having directed the Mau Mau movement, such charges were never proved.

Julius Nyerere;
On his return to Tanganyika, Nyerere was forced by the colonial authorities to make a choice between his political activities and his teaching. He was reported as saying that he was a schoolmaster by choice and a politician by accident. Working to bring a number of different nationalist factions into one grouping he achieved this in 1954 with the formation of TANU (the Tanganyika African National Union).

<u>*Kwame Nkrumah - Ghana*</u>
He formed in June 1949 the new Convention Peoples' Party (CPP), a mass-based party that was committed to a program of immediate self-government. In January 1950, Nkrumah initiated a campaign of "positive action," involving nonviolent protests, strikes, and noncooperation with the British colonial authorities.
<u>*Patrice Lumumba;*</u>
After his release, he helped found the Mouvement National Congolais (MNC) party on 5 October 1958, quickly becoming the organization's leader.

This group of youth, as scholars self-politicised by 1955, while they worked at the Drum, rolling and reading the magazines, seeking Dignity and Freedom.

The Sharpeville Massacre is not covered by Drum Magazine, even though they had two eye-witnesses on the ground. Jim Bailey, the owner of Drum, did not approve the publication of any reports of the Sharpeville massacre, his Father, Sir Abe Bailey, a diamond tycoon, the family and business links to the economy, in my opinion, influenced this decision.

Today, as we discuss Drum's failure to contribute to the Africanist struggle, failure to remove white rule when it should have been removed, John laments,

"I must stop my songs of praise for the Drum Magazine."

Sharpeville Massacre:

March 21, 1960, the Sharpeville Massacre, the turning point in South Africa's history?

Today I ask of those who supported the Charterists between 1955 and 1960, "Why did this incident not force the United Nations to remove the Nationalist Government?"

On November 1, 1958, the Africanists are forcibly removed form the ANC, the ANC now represents the people that are supportive of the Economic Democracy, phase one of the destruction of the Africanist radical and revolutionary path, has been achieved, without the intervention of Government.

On April 6, 1959, the PAC launches, during 1959 their first campaign, the Status Campaign is successful.

The Status Campaign targets the Business Sector, forcing trading stores to open their business to the African, both the Government and the Economic Sector take note of the 'black youth contingent' that is attached to the PAC.

65% of the young black Soweto youth are PAC supporters, self politicised.

In December 1959, the PAC announced that it was planning to initiate a campaign against the pass laws with the aim to free South Africa by 1963.

Linked to this anti-pass campaign, was the £1 per day demand, which would have doubled wages on many of the Africans, this would have been enough to disturb the economic sector.

January 21, 1960, nine police officers are killed in Cato Manor, not directly linked to the Africanist revolutionary, but sufficient to allow the Security forces, and all Globalization Participants, to use the deaths of the nine police officers, as a motivation for any action, they believed would be needed to remove the Africanist.

On 16 March 1960, Sobukwe wrote to the Commissioner of Police, Major General Rademeyer, stating that the PAC would be holding a five-day, non-violent, disciplined, and sustained protest campaign against pass laws, starting on 21 March.

The campaign was made known on March 18, 1960. Circulars were printed and distributed to the members of the organisation and on the March, 21, 1960, a Monday, in obedience to a resolution they had taken, the members of the Pan Africanist Congress surrendered themselves at various police stations around the Country.

At the press conference Sobukwe emphasised that the campaign should be conducted in a spirit of absolute non-violence and that the PAC saw it as the first step in Black people's bid for total independence and freedom by 1963[8]. Sobukwe subsequently announced that:

African people have entrusted their whole future to us. And we have sworn that we are leading them, not to death, but to life abundant. My instructions, therefore, are that our people must be taught now and continuously that in this campaign we are going to observe absolute non-violence.

On the morning of March 21, 1960, Robert Sobukwe left his house in Mofolo, with a groups of supporters, one of them, John Mahapa,[9] and began walking to the Orlando police station. Along the way small groups of people joined him.

---

[8] *Cape Times*

[9] *See page 153*

In Pretoria a small group of six people presented themselves at the Hercules police station. In addition other small groups of PAC activists presented themselves at police stations in Durban and East London. However, the police simply took down the protesters names and did not arrest anyone.

Kaalvoet Theory[10];

The campaign is made known, on Friday 18, March, in 1960, communication links are very difficult, pamphlets are distributed over three days maximum, and thus the small turnout.

**

Robert Sobukwe led the small group of supporters to Orlando Police Station, where they intended to give themselves up for arrest, hoping that his leadership will inspire other Black South Africans to do the same during the next 5 days.

When Robert Sobukwe's group reaches Orlando Police Station at 08:00, he was in the lead, and the Police took him and other leaders into the station, they were released and joined the followers outside.

At approximately 09:00 the Police arrested Robert Sobukwe and his followers, and they were charged with

---

[10] *My theory based on analysis of information available*

sedition, Sobukwe first taken to his home to search for documents, and then to the cells.

Robert Sobukwe and his followers, including John Mahapa, were sentenced to 3 years hard labour, and the PAC executive members to 2 years.

Kaalvoet Theory;

It is 09:00 on the morning of March 21, 1960, all Robert Sobukwe has done, is to organise and lead less than 300 of his followers to present themselves at various Police Stations for arrest in a peaceful civil disobedience campaign, and he is sentenced to 3 years hard labour, for inciting people to rebel against the State.

In May 1963, at the end of the 3 years period, Sobukwe is held on Robben Island under the Sobukwe Clause for another 6 years, then, when ill, banished to Kimberley under house arrest.

As we go through the Sharpeville incident, I believe that the State structured this massacre, and therefore, Robert Sobukwe needed to be incarcerated to prevent detection of their planned action.

The Sharpeville Massacre, gave reason to permanently incarcerate Robert Sobukwe in solitary confinement.

Kaalvoet Alternative Theory to the above;

The Colonizer, has had great skills in creating a villain, out of a fairly reasonable person, turning him into a martyr, a hero, that, when released, will allow the subjugated, to celebrate him, as their Freedom Fighter.

Nelson Mandela's incarceration, and his release, shows a very structured creation, and release of the struggle hero, while hiding, the fear or concern that the Government had for the second protagonist, Robert Sobukwe.

Jomo Kenyatta, appears to have been sentenced, to instigating the Mau Mau rebellion, without any evidence against him. During the trial, he made a statement that compares with the Nelson Mandela Rivonia Trial statement. He was jailed in a remote area, like Sobukwe, had a clause that allowed the Government to incarcerate him indefinitely, then, when freed, he was flown to his followers, where he denied any guilt, and like Nelson Mandela, he was supportive of the whites and their economy.

When Robert Sobukwe was arrested on March 21, 1960, the system, Government and Globalization Participants, were very aware that the Africanist support was firmly behind Sobukwe, and they would have, indirectly monitored his mindset, assessing whether he was prepared to sellout his principles, for what ever motivation, love and protect the whites.

Robert Sobukwe stayed true to his Africanist principles, allowing the Government to release him without any fanfare in May 1969, even though, he was in theory, they most feared man in South Africa.

I provide a comment by John Vorster, the then Minister of Justice, did they really fear Sobukwe as mush as they claim, or, was it part of a creation, that was still being structured, a failed attempt?

John Vorster the then Minister of Justice (settler colonial justice) claimed that Sobukwe deserved this treatment because he felt he had a mission to deliver his African people from slavery and oppression **and could not be changed from this conviction** "this side of eternity". Vorster further made it clear that he could not treat Sobukwe in the same way as Chief Albert Luthuli the President of the ANC, who was merely restricted within his own area, because, in his words, "Comparing Luthuli to Sobukwe, Luthuli is a lightweight".

In advancing the case for passing the law for indefinite detention of Sobukwe John Vorster had this to say in Parliament: "This clause will be used to keep him there longer .... **For here we are dealing with a person, let me say this, who has a strong magnetic personality, a person who can organise, a person who feels he has a vocation to perform this task, well knowing what methods will be applied".**

Kaalvoet Belief

Having studied the Colonizer's decolonization initiatives, many failed initiatives, today, I am of the opinion that, had Robert Sobukwe changed his philosophy, to accommodate the white economy, that would have allowed the continued subjugation of the blacks by the whites, become a supporter of the Charterists, Robert Sobukwe, would have been our first black President of the Republic of South Africa, as early as 1963.

Vaal Triangle:

Between 06:00 and 08:00 on the morning of March 21, 1960, both at Evaton and Sharpeville Police Stations, PAC anti-pass protestors presented themselves for arrest. The Police refused to arrest them, but invited them to wait for a message form a senior police officer.

In Evaton a few hundred protestors were present at 08:00, names were taken and protestors warned to leave. People heard that the Police would like to talk to the community, so far, an as yet undefined source, so a crowed moved to the Police Station, where a few Police Saracen armoured vehicles, and a contingent of armed Polices were in attendance.

The Police, and Saracen vehicles left around 10:00, and the community returned home.

The Sabre jets, reportedly flying over Sharpeville, flew over Evaton, due to the close proximity of the two Townships, by then the Evaton group had dispersed, allowing the media to report that the Evaton group had been obedient, respectful and understanding of what was required, when responding to the aircraft message.

In Sharpeville, Isaac, a survivor tells the same story about the Police asking them to wait for a message, and they patiently waited.

The Sabre-jets swooped low, they had never seen the planes so low, they were afraid but held their position.

He describes the arrival of Police members, all carrying semi-automatic weapons, and how they were placed at intervals along the barbed-wire fencing facing the people.

8 Saracens are positioned, one by one, facing the people, Isaac recalls that they believed they were going to be shot, and they needed to motivate one another to believe it would not happen.

Isaac confirms that a large section of the community, men woman and children, started to arrive at the Police station, during the arrival of the police.

I am of the opinion that Mama Mocomary's version of the military instructing the community to report to the Police Station and wait for a message, was so timed, to allow the entire scenario to develop.

At one stage, the Police announced that the men should gather at the sports ground, where their protest issues would be discussed, and instructed woman and children to remain behind.

The men refused to obey, understanding that they would die is separated form the woman and children.

As the Sharpeville group developed in numbers, so the Police decided that the Sharpeville crowd was large enough to find reason, that would serve their purposes, to teach them a lesson, best.

Then, a large motor car arrives, and drives into the Police grounds, a tall Police Officer alights, a military type baton tucked under his arm, he walks to the fence and looks at the people. He then moves the baton form out under his arm, and holds the baton vertical, form an outstretched arm.

He paraded down to the furtherest Police man, and slowly marched form Police man to the next, I get the impression that he was inspecting the 'guard'.

Isaac and his brother move away form the fence, looking for something to eat, and as they get a block away, the shooting starts, and they drop to the ground.

****

The following extract is taken form the manuscript "If you don't like it Here, Leave" form an Interview[11] I conducted with a Sharpeville Massacre survivor some 8 years back;

---

[11] *This interview can be viewed on You Tube https://youtu.be/NmBFv-PIWDY*

Kaalvoet Comment:

Having interviewed Dick extensively I find Joe, a Security Branch operative during the 1980s and encourage him to view the interview videos, and the make comment that I could use for the purposes of my research.

He viewed every minute of the videos, and his only comment was;

"No, this guy is lying; it was not the whole community. It was only a small group of youth, used by the communist groups. They were small and insignificant. Even their parents did not support them, we knew the people in the community, they did not support these children".

I had no interest in any communication on camera, but my next stop was Africa Dick's mother, I needed to understand the Security Branch attitude to what they were fighting.

I met with Mama Mocomary in Evaton, she is my age, and she receives me well, after briefly discussing the initiative I was involved in, and briefly introducing Joe,

I asked her if I may interview her about the period 1984 to 1994.

Mama first asked me to switch the camera off; she wished to speak to me about something else. I switched off and anxiously awaited what I thought may be a problem with the interview permission.

To my surprise Mama needed to take me back to 1960 and the Sharpeville Massacre, she was present and her father died in the massacre. We started over and I recorded her reminiscing over the massacre, and while listening I understood just how important this event was in negatively shaping the community in the Vaal Townships. I believe it directly led to the level of violence that these Townships experienced during the 1984 to 1994 period.

<u>You Tube Video Interview, as transcribed:</u>

"1960 there were big fights, fighting for .... There were big (indicating by using her right-hand brushed down her left arm) *a long reference book they call ma'lang ... now that reference book, the people. .. The PAC, they do*

not want that big reference book ... they want the small one....... (louder) then one day there comes the soldiers, they speak, ... they told people, go to the police station, they going to police station, ... we are going to the police station, .. The whole Sharpeville, (stretching her arms out wide, then bringing the hands towards one another and then to her chest, reflecting the entire community.)"

"But they told you to go there".

"Yes... the whole Sharpeville... we sit there, the other they give the children milk, (indicating breast feeding,) *... other they smoke...* (Using her two fingers indicating the smoking action)... *they are sitting like this,* (indicating that they were sitting on the floor),.... *we are looking over there,* (pointing with two fingers, stretching form her eyes out ahead), *looking at the Police station, that they police station will bring something nice for them."* (Mama appears to relax, indicating the relaxed mode during the wait at the police station)

(Mama raises her head looking out to the left, her eyes getting bigger, she lifts her left hand). *"Eleven 'o'clock they shoot ...DOOTH,* (she makes the sound of a cannon type shot) *"... they shoot ... what's wrong now ... they shoot, they shooting peoples, ... they shoot peoples on top of their houses,"* (indicating that people were shot, either where they were on top of their houses, or by people form a raised position) *".... people on top of their houses they fall down,"* (indicating the people dropping to the ground), *"the police the soldiers, ..."* (Here she repeatedly stabs towards the ground with what seems to be a rifle and bayonet, her facial expression still seeing the day before her) *"... make the people die ... they shoot them, they make like this,"* (shaking her body to reflect those on the ground in convulsion), *"they are busy making like this,"* (then stabbing them again, showing the pain she still feels), *"making people die."*

"But were you just sitting waiting?"

"Just sitting waiting, waiting for words that come form the police station, telling right ... we are going to get that reference book, ..." (Indicating by tapping her right hand on her left hand, a much smaller reference book). (Mama sits back), *"no fighting, nothing,"* (indicating her sitting position again) *"we*

were sitting just like this ..." (waving both her arms indicating that they were doing nothing), "*we were doing nothing. No fighting, ... nothing, ... no fighting, we were just sitting,*" (then her arm indicating a throwing motion) "*no stones, nothing,* (swinging her arms in a crossing movement and down) *nothing, but they shoot the people, they shoot the people, form Sharpeville to Vukuvenzelele,.... my mother, ...my mother were sitting her house like this one, that shooting form the police station,* (moving her hands and fingers to indicate machine gun fire) *they shooting in the house, ... other peoples house, ...* (Moving her arms around while indicating the chaos and turmoil of the day, eyes wide open)... *Peoples get out and running ... Schildren... died form that, oooooo......* (Clasping her hands to her face, and shedding a tear while I waited in silence)...... (Swinging her arms in a crossing movement and down with each comment that follows,) *....schildren died ... big people died, wooooooooo......... that ... day... was... hororbl* (the word horrible is chocked by her tears that she is now shedding with her hands covering her face), that *day was horrible, that day was horrible, oooo....*"

I was left uncomfortable in the silence and ask a stupid question in order to continue. "And ... at what stage did you leave the police station, did they chase you away?"

"They don't chase us, (her two hands showing a damping motion form face level down, and then indicating the flight motion) *we run away ... we run away, ... and that thing, DOOTH,* (pointing back over her shoulders to where the artillery was based, and then indicating the path of the bullets moving through them while they were fleeing), *shu 'pu' tu. ...... We run away, people running in the street, going this way, they shoot the people in the back. They shoot the people from the front, they turn back ... they shoot ... they shoot ...there is a road that crosses like this,* (indicating a cross-road) *... they shoot form this side ... they shoot form this side ... they shoot form this side........ The blood of the people was running like this in the street,* (indicating that the blood was flowing and looking for a word to describe the gutter drain) *into........ And going to the dam."*

"And they never said anything?"

"Nothing ..... Nothing till today. No-one says anything..........................."

Mama then goes through details of how the dead were treated, how they were buried, and then, most important, how this community received no support, not even the children who lost their parents.

"No support ... nothing, nothing, even today, nothing."

Kaalvoet Theory;

I had no interest in Sharpeville when the above interview was conducted, I was surprised at her claim that the military had called them to the Police Station.

Today I believe that they were called to the Police Station, with intent, and provide the following motivation.

1: *Sharpeville is not far from the PAC leadership, and had the community given any indication, that the masses that did 'protest' at Sharpeville, were part of the official protest, Robert Sobukwe would have been in Sharpeville.*

2: *Evaton reports indicate that it could have taken place in Evaton, had sufficient people turned up for the slaughter.*

3: *Media reports link the 5000 Langa Flats protestors to the Sharpeville Massacre, to give the impression that the Sharpeville 5000 to 7000 were protestors, but the Langa protestors only gathered at the bus terminus at 17:00, in response to the Sharpeville Massacre.*

4: *In my opinion, the Sharpeville community was led to the slaughter, to teach the Africanist a lesson, to kill Africanism, the opposition to Economic Democracy.*

5: *In my opinion, the Afrikaner Policemen, in the position of strength, would never have felt any fear, and in 1960, the young Afrikaner, policeman, would possibly have shot a protestor that was irritating them, expecting the rest of the Africans to behave, which would have been a typical result.*

6: *Only persons with financial interest, in maintaining influx control, and preventing our blacks from stumbling on the foreign nationals working on the mines, would have wanted to teach the Africanist National a lesson, and the Colonizer had ben dealing with the Africanist Nationalist in Africa, from the 1904s.*

Many people will challenge this version, with the concept that no woman and children were present and that the protestors were a threat, I therefore include a picture, taken as the crowd flee the bullets, woman and children, and no weapons visible?

A witness who supports the interview is Humphrey Tyler, the assistant editor of Drum Magazine, this is his version, first published in the London Observer, March 27, 1960, and this copy, as published in the New York Times, his version has been criticised, and I include for support of the 'peaceful protest';

Ian Berry, a Drum Magazine photographer, arrived with Humphrey Tyler, and he describes the event in a similar fashion.

The failure of Jim Bailey of Drum Magazine, to publish Humphrey Tyler's eye-witness report, is confirmation of the power of the Economic Democracy, the protection of the white economy.

This failure, contributed to the survival of white rule, when the opportunity to change, was on the table.

Humphrey Tyler, assistant editor, Drum magazine...

We went into Sharpeville the back way, behind a grey police car and three Saracens. As we drove through the fringes of the township many people shouted the Pan-Africanist slogan 'Izwe Lethu', which means 'Our Land', or gave the thumbs-up 'freedom' salute and shouted 'Afrika!'.

They were grinning, cheerful, and nobody seemed to be afraid". There were crowds in the streets as we approached the police station. There were plenty of police, too, wearing more guns and ammunition than uniforms".

An African approached" and said he was the local Pan-Africanist leader. He told (us) his organisation was against violence and that the crowd was there for a peaceful demonstration".

The crowd seemed perfectly amiable. It certainly never crossed our minds that they would attack us or anybody".

There were sudden shrill cries of 'Izwe Lethu' - women's voices it sounded - form near the police, and I could see a small section of the crowd swirl around the Saracens and hands went up in the Africanist salute. Then the shooting started. We heard the chatter of a machine gun, then another, then another. There were hundreds of women, some of them laughing. They must have thought the police were firing blanks. One woman was hit about ten yards form our car. Her companion, a young man, went back when she fell. He thought she had stumbled. Then he turned her over and saw that her chest had been shot away. He looked at the blood on his hand and said: 'My God, she's gone!' Hundreds of kids were running, too.

One little boy had on an old blanket coat, which he held up behind his head, thinking, perhaps, that it might save him form the bullets. Some of the children, hardly as tall as the grass, were leaping like rabbits. Some were shot, too. Still the shooting went on. One of the policemen was standing on top of a Saracen, and it looked as though he was firing his gun into the crowd. He was swinging it around in a wide arc form his hip as though he were panning a movie camera. Two other officers were with him, and it looked as if they were firing pistols. Most of the bodies were strewn on the road running through the field in which we were. One man, who had been lying still, dazedly got to his feet, staggered a few yards, then fell in a heap. A woman sat with her head cupped in her hands.

One by one the guns stopped.

Before the shooting, I heard no warning to the crowd to disperse. There was no warning volley. When the shooting started it did not stop until there was no living thing in the huge compound in front of the police station. The police have claimed they were in desperate danger because the crowd was stoning them. Yet only three policemen were reported to have been hit by stones - and more than 200 Africans were shot down. The police also have said that the crowd was armed with 'ferocious weapons', which littered the compound after they fled.

I saw no weapons, although I looked very carefully, and afterwards studied the photographs of the death scene. While I was there I saw only shoes, hats and a few bicycles left among the bodies.

The crowd gave me no reason to feel scared, though I moved among them without any distinguishing mark to protect me, quite obvious with my white skin. I think the police were scared though, and I think the crowd knew it.

****

The Aftermath of Sharpeville:

South Africa's economy collapses, it is baled out by the USA banking system.

One week later, March 30, 1960, the United Nations Security Council meets, 851st meeting, in response to a letter form the African and Asian countries to discuss the Sharpeville Massacre.

The meeting is dominated by whether the discussion should be allowed or not, many countries trying to avoid the atrocities that occurred in their own back-yard.

I extract only the minute items that are relevant to the Kaalvoet Theory.

61:   *The Union Government has already arranged for full judicial inquiries to be made to obtain with utmost speed, an official account of the facts. The Government is also considering the appointment of a commission, with a judge as chairman, to inquire into the contributory factors and to deal with the broader aspects of the problem. But even at this early stage, the statement about the alleged mass killing, of "unarmed and peaceful demonstrators", a statement on which the inclusion of this question is based, cannot go unchallenged.*

62.   *Because of this statement and the many mis-leading reports which have appeared abroad, I feel compelled to give the Council, for its information only, the salient features of the situation. I emphasize that I am doing this solely for purposes of information and without prejudice to the Union Government's legal position, a position to which the Union Government adheres as strongly as ever. The history of the disturbances, as it has thus far been authoritatively established, is as follows.*

63.   ***A splinter organization of extremists*** *had started some time ago to organize a mass demonstration to protest against the carrying of reference books. In passing, I might mention that the reference book was instituted when the pass system — which incidentally had been in*

operation for over a century-was abolished in 1952. The reference book consists of: First, an identity card which, under our laws, applies to male and female of all races-not only to the Bantu; secondly, a section which makes provision for noting particulars of tax payments, influx control, etc. The latter is a measure designed to counter uncontrolled flocking of unskilled labour form the rural areas to the industrial areas, where, if it is not controlled, it will create tremendous social problems, housing problems and also have a **depressing effect on wages.**

<u>Kaalvoet Comment;</u>

Few South Africans appreciate that the control of black peoples movements was introduced by the English in 1902. Included was the monthly payment of taxes.

The system, and here I include the mining industry[12], has always manipulated effect on wages. The mining industry created the migrant worker principle, and brought 56% of their Total Labour Force in form outside South Africa, and for this reason, it was essential that the employment activities of the employer, was not exposed to scrutiny form hungry eyes.

---

[12] *Consider the Verdict; Cedric de la Harpe*

In 1870, an African valued his daily rate, at £70 p.a, in 1930, the Gold Mining Industry, was still only paying £30 p.a.

This extraction of profits, using foreign nationals, would never have happened, if it was not for the control on movement by the South African blacks

64. *The essential aims of the reference book are: (a) to afford a means of identification to people, many of whom are unaccustomed to Western life and often illiterate; (b) to provide a ready means of identifying Bantu people form other countries and territories who flock to the Union in large numbers, mostly without any passports or identification papers whatever.*

<u>Kaalvoet Comment;</u>

The investors in South Africa, the English and Americans, through the mining industry, implemented the pass system, and the foreign nationals, were moved in and out of South Africa by the mining industry.

65. *By intimidating and threatening persons who do not belong to the group, the extremists managed to gather a crowd of approximately 20,000 people in a township, Sharpeville, in the Transvaal and a*

crowd of about 6,000 at Langa in the Cape Province.

Kaalvoet Comment;

The 20 000 people is grossly overstated, and must be condemned.
It is alleged that the 'splinter' group of extremists were involved, imagine how large that splinter was, if they could move 20 000 people in Sharpeville.

66. *Police were in the areas concerned to exercise normal control, if needed, as is done in all well- ordered societies all over the world when large masses of demonstrators gather. At Sharpeville some agitators immediately adopted a threatening attitude towards the police. Attempts were made to arrest some of the violators, but the crowd became more belligerent and the police were attacked with a variety of weapons: pangas, axes, iron-bars, knives, sticks and firearms.*

Kaalvoet Comment;

Over the years I have heard people say that they are embarrassed to be South African, today, I am embarrassed as a white South African for this exaggeration, this lie.

But then, then, we saw this repeat itself in Marikana.

69. *Indeed, shots were fired at the police before the police returned fire in order to defend their own lives and also to forestall what might have led to even greater and more tragic bloodshed. I need hardly say how deeply the Union Government regrets that there was this tragic loss of life.*

70. *The action that the police were forced to take must be seen against a background not known to many people outside South Africa. Not two months before the latest tragedy. a group of Nine policemen was brutally battered to death by a so-called "unarmed" peaceful group. On another occasion a party of five policemen was engaged in collecting and destroying about thirty tons of the narcotic. here known as marijuana, which had been collected in a routine inspection. While they were destroying the marijuana, they were set upon by an angry mob which had gathered, and all five policemen were killed and their bodies mutilated by a mob armed with sticks and axes.*

<u>Kaalvoet Comment;</u>
I repeat, the Cato Manor tragedy was not related to the pass protests, it was not the same

circumstances, but was used to motivated a good reason to massacre people, as a warning to others. The Marikana Massacre some 50 years later is typically accepted by many as warranted, because of the killing of policemen.

71.   *I am referring to these incidents merely to point out to members of the Council that, while it is easy, when 10.000 miles removed, to criticize the authorities for having used fire-arms on this occasion, it is indeed asking too much of a small group of policemen to commit suicide. to stand by idly awaiting their turn to be stoned to death. The police all over the world have a difficult and dangerous. and often a rather thankless. task to perform. Surely not only the rioters are human; the police are too, and they have an elementary right to defend their lives when threatened by mobs not amenable to the ordinary methods of control.*

72.   *No Government can allow hundreds of thousands of its citizens to be intimidated by extremists-as the Bantu in South Africa often are-to be threatened with the most dire consequences, if they proceed with their daily occupations and disobey the instructions of a militant group.*

73. *I have with me here a London daily newspaper which is and has been very outspoken in its criticism of the Union Government, Concerning the intimidation practised by mobs against their peaceful fellow-beings who are attempting to carry on their daily lives. the paper says that mobs of strikers roamed the ill-lit streets of African locations outside Johannesburg and rammed sharpened bicycle spokes up the nostrils of African workers riding in strike-breaking taxis. and that the strikers tore up passbooks, returning* only the page with the owner's photograph on it-and beat up the strike-breakers who carried it.

74. *I may add that the demonstrators, far form peaceful as so many believe-and this, I think, is particularly relevant to the inclusion of this item in the agenda-in fact engaged in looting. arson destruction of property, including their own churches, schools and clinics. They cut telephone wires, set buildings on fire, murdered a coloured driver and set his car on fire and stoned civilian people*

<u>*Kaalvoet Comment;*</u>
Looting took place in Evaton, where white businesses were exposed to the protesting crowd.

The people present in Sharpeville claim that no "looting or arson destruction of property, including their own churches, schools and clinics. They cut telephone wires, set buildings on fire, murdered a coloured driver and set his car on fire and stoned civilian people" took place.

My research shows no confirmation of these allegations in Sharpeville.

As the years pass, this type of demonstration will become part of the demonstration, we must ask, 'does this type of protest, have its origins in the system, falsely attaching this actions to defending their violence'

I will leave the balance of the South African statement to the Council for comment after item 80:

75. *This past Monday was ordered by the extremists to be a day of mourning. But what was it in fact? Merely a repetition of the previous violence, plundering and senseless destruction of social and educational institutions which are there for the benefit of the Bantu themselves. But the extremists*

do not mind what they destroy, as long as they do destroy.

76. *Members of the Council may also be interested in certain pamphlets which, according to press reports, were distributed by those behind the riots in Johannesburg. One for example, and I quote it as reported;*

"The present capitalistic South African State must be completely destroyed and a people's State must be built up. Our comrades would want that we wrest the country form our oppressors with armed force and that after victory we march on to the establishment of the South African People's Republic of the world unite! "

77. *It must be clearly understood that the South African Government fully intends to discharge its duties to maintain public order and safety and to safeguard the internal security of the country, whoever may threaten it-white or non-white.*

78. *One of the most important principles involved in this matter is the question of the observance of the law of the land. The point at issue is not whether there is agreement or disagreement with any particular law. The point at issue is that the law*

must be enforced despite disagreement, and no Government worthy of the name. could abdicate form or share its responsibility in such enforcement. If such abdication or sharing does take place chaos will undoubtedly result and rule by the mob will take the place of rule by the Government. The Government itself is the arbiter of the measures it deems necessary to secure obedience to the law, and interference, form any source whatsoever, in this prime responsibility of any sovereign government, cannot be countenanced. Indeed, any such interference, or attempt at interference, could only have a most deleterious effect on the observance of the rule of law-and this applies not only to South Africa. It is equally applicable to all countries and to all the Governments of the world.

79. *Therefore, if by word or deed, or even gesture, this Council disassociates itself form this vital principle of constitutional government, namely the enforcement of the law of the land, a step will have been taken the consequences of which cannot be foreseen.*

80. *It is my Government's belief that the annual discussion of the racial problems of South Africa since 1946 has helped to inflame the situation*

there. It would be even more serious if the present discussion in the Council were to embolden the agitators or serve as incitement to further demonstrations and rioting in South Africa, with subsequent attacks by rioters not only on members of the police, but also the mass of peaceful citizens of all races trying to carry on a normal life. I am instructed to say that if this were to be the result the blame will rest squarely on the shoulders of the Security Council. I am sure that members of the Council would not wish to accept such a heavy responsibility. This question now having been placed on the Council's agenda, it is incumbent on me to report to my Government for instructions.

Kaalvoet Comment;

I started this Chapter, Sharpeville Massacre, with the following question;

March 21, 1960, the Sharpeville Massacre, the turning point in South Africa's history?

Before we look at item 75 in the Security Council minutes, I wish to present my understanding of the impact that the split between the Charterists and the Africanists have on the Apartheid Government maintaining control of the country, beyond 1960:

The Charterists Voice;

The criticism by the Charterists of the PAC March 21, 1960, anti-pass protest, give substance to the white Government's gross misrepresentation of the facts related to Sharpeville;

I present the Charterists attitude to the protest through Nelson Mandela's version[13]:

THE DECEMBER 1959 ANC annual conference was held in Durban during that city's dynamic antipass demonstrations. The conference unanimously voted to initiate a massive countrywide antipass campaign beginning March 31.

>

The PAC at the time appeared lost; they were a leadership in search of followers, and they had yet to initiate any action that put them on the political map. They knew of the ANC's antipass campaign and had been invited to join, but instead of linking arms with the Congress movement, they sought to sabotage us. The PAC announced that it was launching its own antipass campaign on March 21, ten days before ours was to begin.

---

[13] *Long Walk to Freedom; Nelson Mandela 33*

No conference had been held by them to discuss the date, no organizational work of any significance had been undertaken. It was a blatant case of opportunism. Their actions were motivated more by a desire to eclipse the ANC than to defeat the enemy.

<u>Kaalvoet Comment;</u>

The Charterists criticise the PAC for jumping the gun, not allowing sufficient planning to take place, almost giving the white police confirmation that they were right.

Four days before the scheduled demonstration, Sobukwe invited us to join with the PAC. Sobukwe's offer was not a gesture of unity but a tactical move to prevent the PAC form being criticized for not including us. He made the offer at the eleventh hour, and we declined to participate.

On the morning of March 21, Sobukwe and his executive walked to the Orlando police station to turn themselves in for arrest. The tens of thousands of people going to work ignored the PAC men.

In the magistrate's court, Sobukwe announced the PAC would not attempt to defend itself, in accordance with their slogan "No bail, no defense, no fine." They believed the defiers would receive sentences of a few weeks. But Sobukwe was sentenced not to three weeks' but to three years' imprisonment without the option of a fine.

The response to the PAC's call in Johannesburg was minimal. No demonstrations at all took place in Durban, Port Elizabeth, or East London.

But in Evaton, Z. B. Molete, ably assisted by Joe Molefi and Vusumuzi Make, mustered the support of the entire township as several hundred men presented themselves for arrest without passes.

<u>Kaalvoet Comment;</u>
The response to the PAC's call in Johannesburg was minimal. No demonstrations at all took place in Durban, Port Elizabeth, or East London.

This comment confirms that the concept that the PAC call, could never have generate 7000 protestors in Sharpeville.

In Evaton, 'mustered the support of the entire township, as several hundred men presented themselves for arrest without passes', confirms my theory.

Cape Town saw one of the biggest antipass demonstrations in the history of the city. In Langa township, outside Cape Town, some thirty thousand people, led by the young student Philip Kgosana, gathered and were spurred to rioting by a police baton-charge. Two people were killed. But the last of the areas where demonstrations took place was the most calamitous and the one whose name still echoes with tragedy: Sharpeville.

<u>Kaalvoet Comment;</u>

This link of the Langa protest, in most of the media reports, gives substance to the concept that the PAC succeeded in arranging the angry anti-pass protestors in Sharpeville.

The Langa protestors, maybe only 1000-5000, presented themselves in response to the Sharpeville Massacre, at 17:00 gathered at the Langa Flats bus terminus around 17h00 on 21 March 1960.

This group would have been black people protesting the massacre, not directly linked to the anti-pass protest.

Sharpeville was a small township about thirty-five miles south of Johannesburg in the grim industrial complex around Vereeniging. PAC activists had done an excellent job of organizing the area. In the early afternoon, a crowd of several thousand surrounded the police station.

The demonstrators were controlled and unarmed. The police force of seventy-five was greatly outnumbered and panicky. No one heard warning shots or an order to shoot, but suddenly, the police opened fire on the crowd and continued to shoot as the demonstrators turned and ran in fear. When the area had cleared, sixty-nine Africans lay dead, most of them shot in the back as they were fleeing. All told, more than seven hundred shots had been fired into the crowd, wounding more than four hundred people, including dozens of women and children. It was a massacre, and the next day press photos displayed the savagery on front pages around the world.

On Nelson Mandela's comment on the Sharpeville Massacre, I comment as follows:

1:   PAC activists had done an excellent job of organizing the area.

This comment, can only carry substance, if presented as evidence after the Langa incident, which takes place at 17:00 in response to the Sharpeville massacre.

2:   a crowd of several thousand surrounded the police station;

This comment excludes the large number of woman and children that had been gathered for hours, allowing the impression that the police may have been under threat.

Item 75: This past Monday, March 28, 1960; as reflected by Nelson Mandela[14];

*A small group of us — Walter, Duma Nokwe, Joe Slovo, and myself — held an all-night meeting in Johannesburg to plan a response. We knew we had to acknowledge the events in some way and give the people an outlet for their anger and grief. We conveyed our plans to Chief Luthuli, and he readily accepted them. On March 26, in Pretoria, the chief publicly burned his pass, calling on others to do the same. He announced a nationwide stay-at-home on **March 28, a national Day of Mourning and protest for the atrocities at Sharpeville.** In Orlando, Duma Nokwe and I then burned our passes before hundreds of people and dozens of press photographers.*

Two days later, on the twenty-eighth, the country responded magnificently as several hundred thousand Africans observed the chief's call. Only a truly mass organization could coordinate such activities, and the ANC did so. In Cape Town a crowd of fifty thousand met in Langa township to protest the shootings. Rioting

---

14 *Long Walk to Freedom; Nelson Mandela 33*

broke out in many areas. The government declared a State of Emergency, suspending habeas corpus and assuming sweeping powers to act against all forms of subversion. South Africa was now under martial law.

<u>Kaalvoet Comment;</u>

This claim by the Charterists that only a truly mass organisation could have coordinate the day of mourning, gives substance to the white governments claim that they were dealing with a small splinter radical groups during the Sharpeville Massacre.

In my opinion, every African would participate in the day of mourning, Charterist and Africanist, no credit due to Charterist.

Had the Charterists, not wished to discredit the Africanist, and adopted a united African day of mourning, white rule would have been removed, between 1960 and 1963?

This was the time to unite the Africanist again, every Africanist would have celebrated the united Africanist movement, and even the Globalization Participants would have been trumped.

This was the time for the ANC and Nelson Mandela, to support Robert Sobukwe and the PAC's every action, and to have condemned the Sharpeville Massacre, calling for the removal of white rule, but in true European culture, once you have had a taste of being a Globalization Participant, and all the rewards that are promised, it is difficult to share your promised position and rewards with others.

Kaalvoet's inner question to himself;

"Am I wrong?"

******

Project Hammer

Kaalvoet alleges that the wealth of the world, control and give direction to South Africa's political future, in 2013, I discovered this 'far fetched conspiracy theory' and ignored it, as a white South African, I could not believe that Project Hammer was possible.

But, while I am alleging that Nelson Mandela sold the African out, in my new status of African, I find that all theories known to me, should be shared, as I share myself, therefore I share this email blog.

https://blikskottel.wordpress.com/2012/03/05/project-hammer-were-sas-whites-sold-out/

Project Hammer, were SA's whites sold out?
I do not know if what you read here is the truth. I would however like to know if it is or is not.

PROJECT HAMMER:
Project Hammer was a desperate undertaking by the USA government to rescue some of its major banks, who, by the end of the 1980's, faced insolvency.
These banks included Citibank, HSBC, Chase Manhatten and the Bank of New York.

The project was designed to cipher gold and diamonds as collateral as an emergency buoy for the ailing banks and to put the USA's economy on track again.

It is at this stage that South Africa's De Klerk government entered the fray – as major gold and diamond supplier it was the easiest and cheapest way to rescue the USA banking sector.

Only one small problem: South Africa was in political turmoil with the white rightwing challenging the NP government on all fronts. The best smokescreen Citibank could think upon to move large amounts of money and gold bullion was:

– Create political instability (between the old government and the ANC), then create a political vacuum where dodgy gold and diamond deals could be done without too many questions (maybe even an interim NP/ANC government where the minimum control would facilitate covert gold and diamond movements).

Project Hammer involved the trading of US$13.6 trillion in debentures resulting in a "fallout" of about US$1.1 trillion which was stashed in the Howard Hughes account in Credit Suisse. Obviously, in a project of this size, a lot of organizations had to be involved: The CIA, the FBI, the National Security Agencies of all types, The Pentagon in the broadest sense of it and as such, and the Treasury, Federal Reserve. Nobody got out of the act, everybody wanted to get in the act – for there was lots and lots of money to be made.

EXECUTIVE OUTCOMES, SANDLINE, AND THE STASI:

Another individual who has played a considerable role in Project Hammer is South African, Rolf van Rooyen, who operated a number of business entities including one called "Oceantech" and another called "Eastech International Bank." At one time Van Rooyen worked for South African intelligence and is also believed to have been CIA at the time Project Hammer was in process.Of significance is the fact that General Cocke and van Rooyen knew each other, although Cocke says he only spoke to him on the phone but never "shook hands with him." During a police interview in Germany in 1995, van Rooyen when questioned about Project Hammer responded: "If you are referring to Operation Hamer (sic) it is an extremely large, very delicate operation in co-operation with the authorities of various countries in which Oceantech is involved."

Working alongside van Rooyen was South African intelligence operative Riaan Stander. Both Stander and van Rooyen were board members of the "Eastcorp Syndicate" which boasted almost two dozen other companies in its stable. Included were Intercol Pty, Ltd., Cavo Shipping – which conducted intelligence gathering missions for governments – and Bridge S. A. The latter was registered in Monrovia, Liberia.

According to Peter Goslar, once a close friend of Riaan Stander, other board members of Bridge S. A., were Colonel Tim Spicer and Mick Ranger "of Sandline fame." In a letter written to a Washington law firm involved in a lawsuit involving Project

Hammer, Goslar fingers Bridge S A – and hence van Rooyen and Riaan Stander – as "part of the Executive Outcomes operation."

Eastech International bank was underwritten by a Mexican firm Ro-Mar Pharmaceuticals, a firm claiming to control over $100 billion in gold.

Van Rooyen and Stander entered Eastech into an agreement to purchase 5000 metric tonnes of gold at a discount of 4% from the Second London Fix. This gold was held in the free zone area beneath Zurich's Kloten Airport. Interestingly, the contract , which ran to 6 pages, bears the official stamp of the Swiss Police, authorising and validating the transaction.

By 1995 Eastech International Bank had begun to hit the radar screen of regulatory authorities around the world that viewed it with suspicion. But by then it seems probable that much of Project Hammer's South African objectives had been fulfilled. Fearing the worse, Rolf van Rooyen left South Africa and travelled to Germany. And according to his one time friend, Peter Goslar, that is where he still lives albeit protected by former members of East Germany's Stasi spy-network.

Rudolph Ignatius van Rooyen; gebore te Kroonstad op 29 April 1959.
ID nommer: 570429 5021 085
Laaste bekende adres: Rheinstern Hotel 1610, Rheinstern, Dusseldorf, Duitsland.
Alias: Rolf Rondine

Director: Eastech International Bank – established in China and underwritten by a Mexican firm. Contact person: Miss Lin Ying, China.

Riaan Stander: security director of Eastech.

Steve Potnak: managing director of Eastech Bank.

Steve Pansegrow: military intelligence officer supplying Eastech with intelligence reports. He also supplied highly confidential information to C1 in the names of Eugene de Kock and Pieter Botha. Pansegrow's wife was a receptionist for Van Rooyen and Stander.

Irma Els: operator helping in Ifafa (Eastcorp).

Fanie Smith: operator who signed validation certificates for Eastcorp.

• Letter of credit number 9022101 signed by Fanie Smith and honoured by the bank and with a revenue stamp of the Greek government.

• Certificate of deposit of $5 million, stamped by Greek government, signed by Fanie Smit.

• Certificate of deposit of $25 million, stamped by Greek government, signed by Fanie Smit.

• Directors of Eastcorp and Intercol as at the registrar of companies:

Rolf van Rooyen, Rian Stander, Douglas Randell. Intercol: Eugene de Kock, general Tai Minnaar, Pieter Botha. Policemen and members of military intelligence served on both Eastcorp and Intercol.

• Dr HP Bauer – involved with operator "Rosie"; Dr HJ Schuster – agent of FAS in the United States; Julian Rosie – director of FAS in South Africa.

• Riaan Stander liased directly with intelligence officers from C1 (SA Police), namely Eugene de Kock, Chappies Klopper, Pieter Botha and Willie Nortje. They asked help from Eastech to infiltrate rightwing groups in Pietersburg and for help in the movement of large quantities of weapons.

• MAS 57.8.92 Pretoria North case number, investigation officer Lieutenant-colonel AE Botha conducted an investigation into the irregularities – but it was never made public or brought to court.

PART 2: In October 1998 a German intelligence operator forwarded a document marked "Top Secret" to Gerhard Laubscher of the South African National Intelligence Agency, marked MZ/HRB/10-10/98 ser no/IBI citing the disappearance of $223 104 000 008 from the South African economy through "black gold" dealings.

In the report the following 47 persons were named: FW de Klerk, Hernus Kriel, Chris Stals, Japie Jacobs, Org Marais, Anton Rupert, Johan Rupert, James Cross, Christo Wiese (SARB), Christo Wiese (Boland Bank), Dr Swanepoel, Dr Groenewald, Mnr Potgieter, Alwyn Lombard, Jan Lombard, Barend du Plessis, Commissionar Blaauw (Western Cape), Simon Nothnagel, Simon and Peter Nassau, Giel Nieuwoudt, Ben Zuma, Anton Welch, George Hill, BB de Klerk, Chris Nissan, Kobus Kirsten, Van Deventer, Boet Claassen, Big John Smith, Willem Korden/Kordan, Daniel Julius, Jan Koch, John and Faize Adams, Peter Blake, Nick Fourie, Magistrate Liebenberg, Casiem and Shahida Brey, Peter Mopp, Riaan Engelbrecht, Peter Goslar, detective

Justin Swart, Charles/Lester Newton, Robert Ferguson, Wynand Louw.

The report quotes:

"4.7 The RSA has in excess 3000 tons of gold in storage. We cut identify that Cloten in Zwitzerland, Luxembourg and London are used extensively for stored gold.

4.8 The RSA has a small refinery in Switzerland and deals with an other small refinery in Luxembourg (owned be Italian members) to refine gold, remove the tell tale markings on the gold.

4.9 The RSA selling 550 tons of gold every year and approximately 50 tons of gold is stolen every year."

"4.12 Some of this money is then recycled back into RSA

4.13 some examples:
a. The recently announced merger of Goldfields and Gencor.
b. The purchase of BOE, NBS, OK Bazaars etc. by Christo Wiese
c. Old Mutual Bibby Group
d. Gencors Billiton Group
e. Rembrands Richmond Group
f. Anglo Americans Miners Group".

"6.3 High Yield investments goes generally though ABSA, Nedbank, Boland and Standard-Chartered Bank RSA, all with approval from the SARB.

6.4 Arnold van Eck, offshore in;

a. 5, Imposses des Michandes, Veyrier du Lac, 74000 Anmecy-France

b. 9, Bis Avenue D`Albigny, 74000 Anmecy-Le Veux

c. 68, Rue de Billancourt, Beulgne

....

g. Adriaan (Riaan) Stander

h. Switzerland, 17, Rue de Levi,Crans Montana

....

6.5 Van Ecks Associates, Clientel, Co.Directors a.o. are all well known

military intelligence officers and political figures. Large sums of funds

to almost $1,6 billion were handled and controlled by the Van Eck Syndicate on instructions of these politicians and intelligence officers"...............

a. There are in RSA R 37 million in farms unaccounted for

b. R 18 million returned by Van Eck and unaccounted for

c. USD 40 million are being hold in secret accounts in Van Ecks name

d. an unauthorized amount of $6 million was paid to Mrs. van Eck

 e. There are in RSA various assets of enormous value, belonging to Afri-Air, a total of at least R 700 million

 f. Overseas funding in USD 400 million are also unaccounted

 g. a further amount of USD 700 million unaccounted, controlled be Van Eck."

PART 3: Moving money between bank accounts is easy, especially when it is done with the blessing of the major banks and governments; but moving gold and weapons around the globe is not so easy.

Enters one of the key players, shipping tycoon Tony Giordiadis from Greece. Georgiadis had very close ties with Richard Carter (now corporate manager of BMW), the spokesperson for the SA President FW de Klerk. On May 11 and 12, 1990 De Klerk paid an official visit to Greece here he met with President Caramanlis and Prime Minister Mitsosakies.

But De Klerk also met Tony Gordiakis at this time. Of Greek extraction but London based, Georgiadis shipped oil to South Africa in contravention of sanctions and developed close relations with members of the previous government. To distribute money freely, Georgiadis opened a bank account in Liberia for Mallar Incorporated (it was also through this account that bribes to the tune of $22 million were paid to ANC officials during the Arms Deal). Geordiadis's father-in-law Lanaras once served at as director of the shipping firm Alandis.

The conspirators were faced by another huge obstacle: the loyal members of the Defence Force, Military Intelligence, National Intelligence Agency and the South African Police who would immediately put a stop to the transactions should they find out.

Thus followed the most bizarre thing any President of any country has ever done during the past century: FW de Klerk fired all loyal officers so that his collaborators could move freely!

On December 19, 1992 FW de Klerk fired 23 senior army officers – including navy officers who could pose a threat.

"So great was the speed with which De Klerk acted that even the army's public relations office was not informed of the press conference. In addition, many of the officers disciplined were on holiday and were unaware of their suspension. The axed officers included: Major-General Chris Thirion, Deputy Chief of Staff, Intelligence, who had a reputation of being one of the more progressive of the younger generation of generals; Major-General Hennie Roux, Chief of Army Intelligence; Brigadier Ferdie van Wyk, director of Army Communications, who master-minded Project Echoes; Brigadier Tolletjie Botha, Director, Directorate of Covert Collection, which was raided in November by investigators of the Goldstone commission, including UN personnel; Brigadier Oos van der Merwe, Director of Army Intelligence; Commander Jack Widdowson of the Navy."

"He named only three other officers, Colonel At Nel, Col Chris Prinsloo and Commandant Stephan Snyders, who were all put on compulsory leave".

"This followed the purge of 19 police generals in August (see Roca Report no 45) as part of a drive to bring the police in line with the negotiation process. The Further Indemnity Act pushed through Parliament in August, needed to help ease officers out. The November raid on Military Intelligence's Directorate of Covert Collection in November by Goldstone investigators which provided the pretext for setting up the probe headed by Gen Pierre

Steyn. A top-level meeting between senior Umkhonto we Sizwe (MK) and SADF officials in early August, brokered by the National Intelligence Service, which generally carries out the will of the cabinet. December's "rationalisation " measures which include the retrenchment of 6000 middle ranking officers."

In just five months De Klerk has opened the door wide for his own operators to continue the sell-out. " I have never before seen a government destroy its own power base such as this one is doing, " said former chief of Military Intelligence, Gen Tienie Groenewald. " while the country is steadily moving towards complete chaos, the government has effectively neutralized the SADF's intelligence capabilities by removing the eyes, ears and nose of its defense forces. "

The Greek shipping tycoon could now go about his business unhindered. Georgiadis was off course also implicated in the swindle with the sinking of the Greek ship, Salem, off the African coast earlier in what was described by Loydds of Great Britain as the biggest maritime swindle ever:

"SALEM: Lloyd's pursues what may be the biggest maritime swindle ever At 10:50 a.m. Greenwich time on Jan. 17, crewmen aboard the tanker British Trident sighted a ship in distress off the coast of Senegal in northwest Africa. The Salem, a 214,000-ton supertanker, registered in Liberia, was listing and dead in the water. By radio contact with the tanker, Trident learned that a series of mysterious explosions was responsible for the disaster; indeed, a cloud of orange smoke billowed from the tanker's deck.

By 11:30 the disabled ship's Greek-born captain, Dimitrios Georgoulis, and his 22 crewmen, most, of them Tunisians, had…"

• SIDE NOTE: It was at this time that the whole Project Hammer was put at risk by FW de Klerk's impulsiveness: German operators learned that De Klerk was having an affair with Georgiadis' wife, Elita (Lanaras' daughter). A memorandum was sent to the CIA, who decided to put a lid on the affair until after the completion of Project Hammer. Knowledge of the affair would not only open the can of worms, but it was not clear what Georgiadis' reaction to the affair would be. It thus only became public after another two years.

• But there was a twist: Marike de Klerk. When FW de Klerk divorced Marike to marry Elita, a clause was written into the divorce agreement that De Klerk would be able to censor any books or articles Marike decided to write – which indeed he did when he prevented the publication of a chapter titled Grotgesprek (Cave Conversation) in the autobiography titled 'n Plek Waar Die Son Weer Skyn (A Place Where The Sun Shines Again).

But Marike de Klerk was not done yet. Then, sadly, on 2 December 2001 she was brutally murdered in her Dolphin Beach Complex, Bloubergstrand apartment hours after sending an undisclosed fax to Holland.

Curiously – the European Union paid R30 000 into the account of the murder accused Mboniswa channelled by the Foundation for Human Rights for DNA tests.

Mboniswa stood trial in the Western Cape High Court in CASE NO CC 101/2002b and was found guilty of the murder of Marike de Klerk without taking the stand in his own defence.

German filmmaker Ziri Rideaux is currently getting ready to shoot the feature film Project Hammer in Johannesburg, South Africa, a political suspense thriller based on her true story as a journalist.

Blikskottel: Does not know the truth, but if this is all true, the whole new RSA is one big farce.

KAALVOET COMMENT:

I would like to say I don't believe it, but maybe, if I had great wealth, and the blacks were going to take over, before they stuffed the country up, if I was in the position to get involved, I may have taken advantage of the transition.

It is with great reluctance that I refrain from further comment, however, my inner question is whether this theory was heard by our ANC leaders, and thus their corruption?

For four years I carried this burden of knowledge with me, even if it is a conspiracy theory, an African would share it around his family clan.

***

The African has still not been freed.

For years, my wife Nettie and I have worked towards developing tourism in the Township and Rural Villages, receiving no support from the media, or any of the Tourism Bodies, including South African tourism, mainly because the concept of these industries, is entrenched in the mindset, that you do not expose your international visitors to risk, and risk resides in the black areas, swart gevaar, is still so deeply entrenched, in our 'suburban mindsets'.

Some 12 years back, I developed 10 'shack accommodation' rooms, in the backyards of residents in Orlando East, the Sowetan published an article, and John Robbie, Radio 702 presenter, while covering the morning Newspapers, had the following to say:

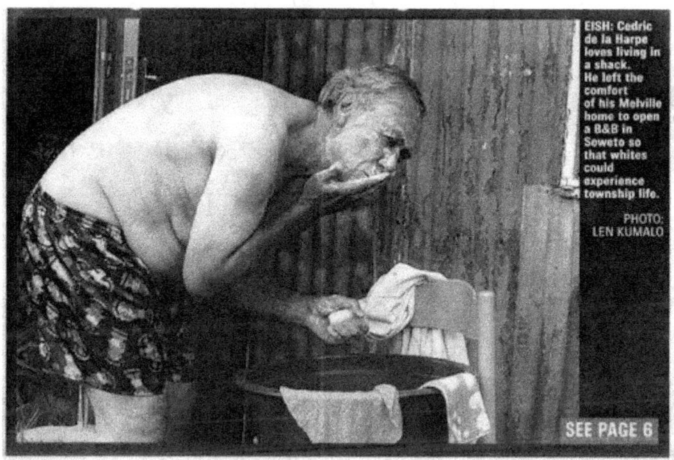

"Look at this white guy, wants to charge visitors R 400 to sleep in a shack, just so that they can be mugged."
I was furious, my email, in which I accuse John Robbie of being a racist, he does not answer, his producer Jonathan does, I rant and rave, Jonathan apologises, and says that John's comment was tongue in cheek.

John Robbie, no racist comment can be deemed to be tongue in cheek.

Over the next years, I regularly invite Mr. and Mrs Robbie to share some of our experiences, and he just ignores the invite, so does every other travel journalist or radio presenter, they all avoid getting into a position, where they may be tempted to make a personal decision on whether the Township streets are safe enough for white people to walk through, it remains their corporate policy, that still dictates swart gevaar.

From 2005, we have offered home-stay in Townships and Villages all over the Country, at great cost to Nettie and I, the intention was not necessarily the international tourist, to whom we extend our many thanks and appreciation, but to give the South African wishing to visit the Kruger National Park, the facility of driving towards one of the Kruger gates, detouring into a local village, and arrange a magic night's accommodation, or even a few nights, with a family homestay visit, while driving through the Kruger Park during the day. It is also possible to enjoy the Kruger National game drives from the nearest gate.

The Kruger National Park, and the tourism sector, gives no support to our initiatives, all aimed at empowering the still subjugated.

Year after year, we introduce new initiatives, and the media and tourism never accept an invitation to assess.

Their message with regard to these dangerous areas, that is sent to the rest of the world, is the same attitude that is filtered into the white South African community, *"it is not safe to walk in these areas"*

During 2017, we publish a guide book, "Passport to Soweto", we drive the publicity and invites for months, not a bite from any media, not a bite from South African Tourism, Gauteng Tourism, or Johannesburg Tourism,

"Passport to Soweto" with tourism support, with a little media support, could empower an entire community, economically.

Nettie and I worked with the Orlando East community for six months, meeting weekly, planning, development, and as the tourism industry fail to respond, a few months back, I go into self imposed exile, embarrassed at our failure, my failure.

While in exile, the only question I ask of those who will listen, is;

"Why do you never find a journalist, any media, the Tourism sector, give a positive comment to the tourist, with regard to the safety of Soweto streets, if entering unguided?"

The answer is very simply, 'Swart Gevaar', the mining industries political cries, that has protected the wealth of the world since the 1940s, and still rests in every structure, I always knew the answer, but believed that we could break through.

Then March 16, 2018, the Minister of Police introduces us to the SAPS latest Public Order Policing initiative,

As part of efforts to stamp the authority of the state, the South African Police Services has unveiled the national Public Order Policing (POP) reserve units.
The launch saw the units being capacitated with human and physical resources to enable the police to mitigate situations in respect of crowd management and violent community protests in the country as well as the SADC region.

"Strengthening the existing POP units will ensure democratic policing under the Bill of Rights which guarantees that everyone has the right to peacefully and unarmed assemble, demonstrate, picket and present petitions," National Police Commissioner General Khehla Sitole said.

At present, 41 POP units consist of four reserve units and 37 provincial units exist.

"The full implementation of the POP enhancement and capacitation process will result in four established national reserve units and 50 provincial units, with a staff compliment of approximately 11 000 members," Sitole said on Friday.

The Public Order Policing unit, is supported by all, it brings back the comfort that the Apartheid police brought to the white community.

I have asked myself why the system discourages the integration of white people into the Black areas, particularly the poverty white groups?

The answer is very simple, like Brazil, if we have poverty whites, integrated in the black poverty areas, crime will escalate, but like Brazil, the face of the economy will change, and more opportunities will be created, for both the poverty black, and the white.

For the first time I understand the mindset to keep the whites out of the Township, we will free the blacks from the Public Order Policing control, the police will not shoot protesters, if there are whites integrated in the poverty protest, the white world will not accept it, if a white was shot.

"If I was standing on the Marikana hill, firearm strapped to me side, waving and shouting with the mine labour, no-one would have died that day."

****

<u>*Mindset; Anti-white, or love the white.*</u>

Nelson Mandela and the ANC accepted the 'love the white' concept devised by the Charterists, and this group, with their handlers, generated the concept 'love the white' equals opportunity and income, and used this concept from the mid 1980s to 1994 and beyond, in order to sway the African population, into believing that the ANC vote, based on 'love the white', will bring opportunities, which would ensure the ANC political future, for 20 years to come.

Off this basis, when you debate with ANC elders, when needed they will tell you that the only difference between ANC and the PAC, is that the ANC love the whites, and the PAC hate them.

Kaalvoet offers an extract from Consider the Verdict, where Africa Dick, gives his version of the 1994 Peace Agreement, signed by de Klerk:

****

The next week there is a big meeting in Sebokeng, the Houtkop stadium, Nelson Mandela comes to talk to us.

A few whites from National Party come with, so as Cedric, I am able to sit in the tenth row, I relax, is the war over, maybe I can go home.

"People, I am sorry I took so long to come and meet with you, but I was very busy. I was negotiating this agreement with FW de Klerk, it is now signed, we have won the struggle." He waves a document in his left-hand as he talks to the people. I look at Dick, Quagga, Adolf, Richard, Jimmy, they are all sitting near the front, not showing any excitement, their struggle has been a war, Mandela is ignoring them, he is giving them no credit for their fight, for the part they played in destabilising our country.

"FW de Klerk, in this agreement, says you people must put your weapons away, stop fighting, stop killing, we must make peace with the whites, we must love the whites, they also belong, it is also their land. If you vote for me, put a cross against my picture, you will put me in Government, with de Klerk, and then, they will give you free education, jobs, houses, electricity, stoves, water," I do not hear the end of the promises, the elders behind me are standing, waving their fists in the air, shouting "Viva ANC, Viva Mandela, Viva ANC, Viva Mandela."

Viva ANC, Viva Mandela, Viva ANC, Viva Mandela."

Dick's mother my Carer, ignore us, the elders are in celebration, they are drinking beer.

When we get home, we are summoned; we are instructed that we will sleep at home, no longer on the streets. Our firearms are taken away from us, our fathers bury them, we help dig the deep holes, bury the firearms in plastic and tins.

"Dick, you must not fight with the amaBoere, we win, we give you education, we give you jobs, you must love the whites, you must forgive the whites."

****

During the final scenes showing 1994 peaceful elections, I take the opportunity to talk to the Members of the Jury.

"Sirs, when we put ourselves into the position of the complainants, if I was a still disadvantaged black youth today, I would be asking whether our struggle icon, Nelson Mandela was conned by the National Party, or whether some 'financial force', 'bought' the ANC leadership, resulting in the de Klerk promises, in exchange for banning any antipathy towards what I did as a white?"

"Members of the Jury, it took me years before I heard the community blame Nelson Mandela for having failed them. I know he carried the 'piece of paper', that brought us peace, that allowed economic segregation to continue, I ask myself, behind closed doors, 'Was Mandela conned, or was he in collusion?'"

The monitor focus moves back to the 1993 youth, still sitting in the Houtkop Stadium.

The young comrades are still sitting slouched with heads bowed, the elders have spoken, promises have been made, they will hardly benefit, but those born to them will receive their spoils, as Dick would say, "I fight for my children, so they can eat chocolates".

"The elders will always tell the youth 'do not talk like that', silencing any expression of antipathy towards what I did, in exchange for the de Klerk promises, for which us whites are still in debt to many. Our reliance on the lack of antipathy, should give us no comfort."

"Sirs, those members of the Jury, who understand the power of the antipathy expressed by the world after the holocaust, need to understand that the same powers that caused the damage to our African people,

suppresses their antipathy in exchange for a job, a space around the Corporate Boardroom table."

"It is time that we see the evil perpetrated, through the eyes of the victims, as we give them freedom to express antipathy, to what I did."

"Sirs, if you please, we request a postponement, to recover from the evidence presented, and allow our minds to absorb the results of the 1994 Peace Settlement, and the failed promises."

****

<u>Social Violence</u>

The social violence that takes place in our country today, is directly related to the destruction of the community during the period 1984 to 1994, when the youth were destabilising the country.

During the CODESA negotiations, the youth, our 'lost generation', were part of the 'needed' reconstruction and development, and billions was 'budgeted' for their reconstruction.

Having buried their firearms, and pledged the love for the whites, they were no longer a problem, and the money pledged to reconstruct this generation, was used for the building of houses, where tender money could be filtered, and Dick, carried his housing allocation, from 1994, to when he died in 2016, no reconstruction, no housing.

Kaalvoet quotes an extract from the manuscript 'Consider the Verdict'.

"Sirs, even the limited link that you had to the pre-1994 period, will bring back the smell of burnt flesh while you consider the evidence."

"Members of the Jury, in many circles, it is an accepted fact that there in 'no lost generation' in our country, we have been able to convince those who suffered the atrocities that they are 'fine', that they do not need rehabilitation. Saved us billions. Maybe costing billions as we struggle to increase our productivity?"

"We present the motivation for having established that we did not have a lost generation in 1994, and suggest that if that is an accurate reflection, then, maybe we lost a generation since 1994."

"How do we bring together our suburban community with what we experienced in the Vaal

Triangle, the 1984 to 1994 period? As a South African in the suburbs, I did not see this period. How do we repair the damage done to our 'Lost Generation', assuming there is one?"

"Members of the Jury, I ask you to place yourself in the position of those communities, young and old, the necklacing, the smell of petrol and burning tyres, overpowered by the smell of burning flesh, a smell and taste that still lingers in my mouth and nostrils."

"How many children never finished their schooling?

"How many children were involved in crime, first the delivery trucks, then the TV's from our houses?"

"Yes, we asked them to put their weapons down, to love us whites, vote ANC, and we made them promises."

"They buried their weapons, they love the whites, they vote ANC, but the promises have not been met."

"Why were these promises not met, why were the promises to rehabilitate the Lost Generation not met?"

"Because the academics deemed that they did not exist? Or, was the motivation not to spend the money on re-building our youth, that had just come out of the struggle?"

"I will not quote the academics, or the document that I am going to read the following extracts from. I had an opportunity to meet the writer who was penned the following comment, he was disillusioned with the state of our country, and accepted my findings on the Lost Generation."

'The rise and fall of the 'lost generation' is reflected in its elasticity as its size was re-estimated in the early-1990s. In 1991 the 'lost generation' was said to include four to five million people. At one point the figure of six million was given.

"But in 1993, CASE reported that less than half-a-million young people were 'lost' - just five percent of the age group. The waning of the moral panic reflected its contingency; whilst intense for a time, it had little lasting impact."

"Does South Africa have a "youth crisis"?', asked the report of the HSRC research programme in 1994."

The short answer to this question is: No. ... There is no 'youth crisis' as such, but a range of intractable problems within which young people find themselves and that should be addressed in policy.

"Members of the Jury, take note of the initial estimate of the size of the 'Lost Generation', in 1991 it was four million, five million, or six million?"

"For those of you who were in South Africa in 1993, how many of you did not join my family and stockpile your homes with non-perishable food stuffs; we had more on our shelves at home than the super-markets."

"What caused the reduction of the Lost Generation from six million to half million in 1993?"

I sit down; wait for an answer, not expecting an answer. I look at the faces of the controllers, they are all looking down at their lap-tops, possibly studying the full report that I am referring to.

"Sirs, the promises made in 1993 by de Klerk and Nelson Mandela, caused the black youth that were questioned in the survey, to answer positively, to hide all antipathy towards their negative experiences."

"Today still, we will hear a positive answer from any youth, to every question, if you do not give positive a positive answer, you will be excluded."

"Members of the Jury, let me read the results of the survey for you."

The survey conducted the following year by CASE for the JEP also suggested that two out of three young people - in this case of all races, and aged between 16 and 30 - did not fall into their broadly-defined categories of 'marginalised' or 'lost' (CASE, 1993)

"Sirs, how politically correct are we, that in 1993, we survey youth of all races, while the Townships are burning? Surely we should have restricted the survey to the 'marginalised' or lost 'groups'? "

Surveys show that a high proportion of young people participate in religious, sporting, and other organised activities. The CASE/JEP survey reported that more than two out of three young people attend church at least twice a month; only eight percent did not identify with any religion. Many - especially young women - are active in church choirs.

Almost 50 percent of young men are active in sports clubs.

Another survey of young black people found that one-third were active in youth clubs (CASE, 1993:7-8; Moeller, 1991).

"Members of the Jury, the defendants would have used this report to accept that we have no damaged youth in 1994. If they ask you to accept that this survey as valid, then we should ask, who accepts the responsibility for what happened to church attendance since then, 'two out of every three young people attend church at least twice per month'."

"Almost fifty percent of young men are involved in sports clubs."

"Sirs, this is during the period 1991 to 1993. Our Townships were in turmoil. We have fifty percent of young men involved in sports clubs. What has happened to these clubs today? What has happened to these young men?"

"If we did not fail them before, we failed them since 1994, or, are we, as the previously advantaged, claiming that we had these sports clubs in position, when we handed over our country?"

"Sir, this status existed in 1984, when every child played sport, was involved in music, singing, dance, drama. When Dick and the street struggle heroes closed the schools, so formal structured sport and recreational activities disappeared in the Townships."

"What have we, in our New Democracy, done to rehabilitate these activities since 1994?

"Nothing!"

"Today, no structured soccer, takes place at schools in the Township."

"The Bafana-Bafana strength in 1996 came off the school and club level, that existed in 1984. The Bafana-Bafana weaknesses in 2016, comes off the school and club level that exists in 2016."

Surveys also indicate attitudes on the part of young people which suggest low levels of alienation. In the CASE/JEP survey, young people were asked to choose adjectives to describe themselves.

The most frequently given response was 'ambitious', followed by 'happy', 'caring', 'confident' and 'honest'. "The result is a picture of the youth as highly positive in outlook', CASE assessed, 'notwithstanding the majority feeling that they will not be able to fulfil their potential' (CASE, 1993:25).

"In the Key Life Skills courses we give, the choice of positive adjectives that the youth use to describe themselves still exists, and they use them to define their strengths. The school principal will tell you that these children will never admit to any weakness."

"The comment that the children feel they will not be able to fulfil their potential, relates to their weaknesses. In the Key Life Skills courses, the activity allows them to admit to their weakness, and in general, every weakness is directly related to their strength. 'I can sing very well.' 'I am too shy to sing in front of people'."

A study in Natal found that young people faced, on average, a three year waiting period between leaving school and finding their first job (Moller, 1991).

But most young people do, eventually, find employment. One study of Soweto students who left school in 1984 found that fewer than one in five were unemployed seven years later, although almost all had experienced at least one spell of unemployment.

Among students who had left school in 1988, almost half were still unemployed (Bennell with Monyekolo, 1992).

"Sirs, this unemployment trend, established between 1984 and 1988 has continued at the same negative spiral."

"Sirs, there is a Lost Generation; it is still growing due to the failure to rehabilitate it in 1994. Children and grandchildren are only what their parents can give them, all the good, and all the bad."

"Sirs, today we have identified what contributed to the Soweto youth, and others, looting from the Somalis. Why we have violent protests, often including the burning of libraries, challenging our struggle history for education."

*"Members of the Jury, this part of the struggle, even though it is never acknowledged, was a struggle for economic freedom; listen to Dick when he tells you he fought, **'so that his children can eat chocolates'.**"*

"If we had not segregated economically, if we had not allowed economic segregation, this turmoil would never have occurred."

All the politicians who claim they participated in the successful CODESA negotiations, failed the African, with no voice.

***

The anti-white, or love the white, which separates the ANC and the PAC, is the power that today still keeps the various factions of Pan Africanists apart, almost in conflict.

During the past years, I have listened to various PAC supporters discuss whether they should include whites in their group, or exclude them, normally the exclusion would be vocal and anti-white, with 'One Settler, One Bullet' the main debating point.

This manuscript focusses on the Nelson Mandela and the ANC's 'love the white' tactic, Kaalvoet believes, given that the world economic powers were supportive of the NP and the White Capitalist Monopoly controlling our country, in order to protect their wealth, they needed to ensure the acceptance of Nelson Mandela and the ANC's 'love the white' policy, and between the NP, the Economic Sector, and the C.I.A, Kaalvoet believes that the conflict between various faction within the PAC, since 1960, was due to systematic infiltration and manipulation by the security forces.

The ANC loudly claim that their movement was plagued by infiltrators on behalf of the Apartheid Government, why should this not be the case within the PAC?

The close cross-over between MK, and APLA, agents could have infiltrated APLA and triggered the "One Settler, One Bullet' slogan in 1966, the slogan that entrenched the PAC as anti-white, influencing the elders to move from PAC to ANC, in order to participate in the 1994 Peace Settlement promises.

"One Settler, One Bullet" is not African, it does not speak to the African Humanity, this is why the PAC remains separated, it is why the voters avoid PAC, our Country needs to shake off the slogans, that have caused great division in the Country.

Julius Malema, by no means an Africanist, judged by the African 'humanity lifestyle' it is questionable whether he is African, yet he will chant 'Kill the Boer', off the 'One Settler One Bullet' slogan, expressing his hate for the whites, a hate which is directly linked to the PAC, a hate the causes the voters to look away from the PAC, when he himself, will within a day or two, tell the media, who publishes all his comments, as if he is under instruction by the economic sector, that he is not anti-white, he only hates the white supremacist, the Boer.

From an African point of view, who is the white supremacist, the Boer, or the Non-African White Capitalist Monopoly investors, who have controlled the country since 1903, the group who stole the land, the group who stole the minerals?

Malema's attack on the Boer, does not bring him any votes, most of the poverty Blacks are African, many do not want to be associated with any anti-white philosophy.

The verbal attacks on the white, disturbs the Boer / Afrikaner community, as the viscous and violent attacks on farmers and their families, gives them reason to claim genocide.

The Farm Murder situation in our country, is the one aspect that keeps the ANC in power, it keeps all mindsets on the anti-white, or love the white concept, that is directly translated to the Africanist as anti-white, and therefore, to be avoided, it is also seen by many, as the removal of whites from the farms, and the potential of land redistribution.

While in my spiritual exile, I start to see the farm murders, the violent attacks, the disfigurement of the bodies, in a different light, I have always criticised the ANC for treating it as no more than the violent attacks the black people are subject to, then, I wake up to the fact that they are the same, only, as a white, I do not necessarily register the damage done to the blacks, during the viscous attacks, this week the chain-saw attack, yesterday, three blacks on the Punda Maria Road, no more than 3 km from our Village home, murdered, by being tied up in a vehicle, and the perpetrators, firing into the petrol tank, till the car explodes into fire.

This morning, allegations that a SA Police forensic investigator, had himself, sexually abused the children during the investigation, how do we heal a sick society?

We have a lost society, the white farmers no more than pawns in the bigger picture, not part of the fraternity, no different to the black victim, when the perpetrators 'need' arrises, and farmer and his family are in the firing line, they will be attack, robbed, raped and killed, just like his black brothers and sisters are, often many miles away.

We have a lost society, a sick society, that is not Africanist, a society that was splintered by the Coloniser, using Christianity and selective segregation.

The united Africanist Nationalist, a mindset and philosophy, that, had it not been destroyed, would have brought South Africa, Liberty, Equality and Fraternity to all, by 1960, all but those wealthy investors, who had 'stolen' the land, in order to secure our mineral rights.

Having achieved security of wealth by 1902, they entrenched this security, through legislation, that can never be challenged, in their legal structure.

Kaalvoet's theory that this wealth can only remain entrenched, by keeping the whites from integrating into the Africanist community, allows the criminal element to continue attacking the farmer.

Australia, offers support to the white farmers, that would like to farm in Australia, the ANC attack the Australian Government.

An English journalist Katie Hopkins, on February 7, 2018 writes;

<u>Corrupt Members of South African Police Force Facilitate Farm Attacks</u>
I ask the sergeant about this loss of evidence and why the dockets are always "misplaced at the station" or lost in transit.
He says dockets are methodically destroyed either because the police officer knows who the suspects are or the investigating officer is lining his pocket. He tells me about several detectives with 20 to 30 years of experience in investigating crimes who have been fired for selling

dockets, or deleting them for cash; age or number of years in the service are no indicators of loyalty.

Dr. Burger confirms this assertion. He refers me to a recent study in 2016, a doctoral thesis on cash-in-transit robbers who the author interviewed in prison. These criminals were very clear: for a price, it was easy to buy the cooperation of certain police offers.

Services that could be bought included: cooperation with the police to obtain rifles; a police safe house in which to store stolen money; the disappearance of police dockets; the investigating officer agreeing to be less than efficient in his investigations.

It is devastating to realize that corrupt police are willing to equip farm attackers with arms and ammunition, are willing to conceal stolen cash for their cut, and are willing to circumvent justice for cash. I have sat with the victims of these crimes, victims who called the police for help, knowing it was futile and that help would never come.

We have become a country where, crime investigation and prosecution, is poor to say the least, and few of us will contest the allegations that case files are removed from the system through corruption or involvement.

Corruption throughout the system, has become acceptable, and if the politicians and officials, and here I do not exclude the private sector, get away with it, it allows the 'criminal' to extract his share from the people.

During the 1984 to 1994 violence, employment opportunities did not exist, and community income was supported by the youth groups, involved in the 'repossession activities', society closed their eyes to this 'economic activity', and we have done nothing to replace this 'economic activity' to meet the needs of the poverty group.

What is the Africanist's greatest obstacle to achieving the Brotherhood of Man, and freeing Africa?

The obstacle that prevents the unity of the Africanist, is the division entrenched by the mining industry and the Charterists, that wealth comes only to those, who support and protect the western capitalist economy, and in order to do so, a person can't be anti-white.

I have said it before, there in no reason for an African person, not to be anti-white, but there are restrictions to this sentiment, seek out the enemy, the ones who took your land in the late 1870s, not the white face, and you will find unity among the Africanist.

Julius Malema, when he entered the political debate, entered with the concept of nationalizing the mines and banks, it shifted to the Land Invasion / Expropriation without compensation. To Kaalvoet, it is indicative of the fact that we had moved into the 'love the white' mode, where the mining industry, is his protected zone, notice that he does not comment on the Anglo American stance regarding the election of Cyril Ramaphosa.

In April, 2018, he adjusts his attitude further towards the white economy, "Malema says his issue is with white supremacists and not white people in general".

This comment, moves the focus away from the very skilled 'Anglo American' investors, who stole the land in the 1870s, moving their wealth our of the country after 1994, and then disinvests when Jacob Zuma becomes President of the ANC in 2008.

Malema, does not consider that the elite, English, 'Anglo American', achieved the wealth they achieved, due to their white supremacist status, off the Slave Trade. As he moves towards the white economy, he attacks the enemy that the elite have created, the Boer, the proud people, the Boer, very much in the mode of the Zulu, proud and loud, proud of their achievements, the Boers are Malema's enemy, and as he mutters the land invasion concept, so the criminal elements attack the farms with impunity.

Supremacy is the domain of the few:
Without fraternity, liberty would produce the supremacy of the few over the many. Without

fraternity, liberty and equality could not become a natural course of things. It would require a constable to enforce them.

So, our minds remain entrenched in the principle that destroyed the united Africanist nationalist of 1949, 'love the white' at the expense of the African.

The ANC and the EFF presently allow the 'anti-white' concept, attached to the Africanist, off the following attitude:
"Let us sacrifice a few white farmers, while we keep the Africanist in Africa from uniting, while we protect the mining investors, and their accumulated wealth".

Should the 'Africanist' wish to move many of the elder black voters, back towards the Africanist Philosophy, all you need to do, is to make a bold statement, that you are not anti-white, and the most powerful call you can make, is to *"condemn the 'farm murders', in the name of the Africanist's Brotherhood of Man"*, a philosophy that is not 'anti-anyone'?

It will destroy the one weapon that the ANC have used since 1955, and allow the Brotherhood of Man to rekindle.

***

African Economic Reconstruction

The Africanist must not fall into the trap, of playing the game on the fields, and under the rules, of the white capitalist monopoly, who removed your land, using methods that are in conflict with the African culture of land tenure and usage.

The Africanist today, is finding it very difficult to unite, because they are trying to play the Charterists game, the game that separated the Africanist from politics in our country, the game that separated the majority from the economic benefits, that game keeps the majority subjugated.

If the Kaalvoet theory has any merit, by Mandela becoming a Charterist, they selected both the ANC and Nelson Mandela for their future leadership, this allowed the ANC to develop in numbers after 1960, as it allowed the 'elite' and the academic in the ANC, to understand the need to go into exile, to educate and prepare their families, for their position in politics and business, when they were able to join, the white capitalist monopoly system.

Those of you who did not have the opportunity that others had, the still subjugated, will remain subjugated, by this Charterist creation, impossible to unite with the elite, and finding it difficulty to unite, in the Brotherhood of Man.

The 'united' Africanist Nationalist, as remembered by the elders, will only become a Brotherhood of Man, if the common cause that divides us, moves away from the trap of 'anti-white', entrenched by the ANC and their son, the EFF, to one of, that switches our African Economic Reconstruction mechanism, to those 'still subjugated' (SS) by the 'new democracy'.

ANC the selected tribe and their families:
The class, or caste structures, used by the Colonizer, to divide the majority, from their selected tribe, the selected caste or class, to those who will for ever be subjugated, is still entrenched in all the colonies.

In South Africa, this is very visible, not only in colour, but in those who support the ANC 'love the white' economy, and those 1950s Africanists, who allegedly did not 'love the whites', subjugated and abused, never ever given the opportunity, to be considered civilized enough, to be included in the white economy.

For the purposes, strictly to commence the debate, the thought process, Kaalvoet separates our black population into two economic classes, the Now

Advantaged, (NA) and the Still Subjugated, (SS), and provides a few thoughts on how we can all uplift the SS.

Say, the NA is defined as a black family, who own or drive an expensive car, live in an elite previously white suburb, where the parents, or the children, have received their education, at Private Schools, or one of the few good Government Schools, the sort of top 20% of the Government Schools, or, schools that are not in South Africa, or in Universities overseas, not born in South Africa, they no longer qualify for the full 'Black Status' when considering Empowerment, Kaalvoet suggest 50% of the SS value.

Let us, for example consider, the simple to understand process of a sports quota, if the cricket or rugby team, requires a quota of 6 blacks in the team, if the current crop are all out of the NA Class, they would only represent a quota of 3, and immediately, we make space for another 3, out of the SS group. This will take place throughout the Corporate and Government structures, and immediately start allowing the still subjugated, into the employment sector.

Economic Reconstructing;

The African, when united, will reconstruct the economy that they controlled in the early 1900s. In 1930, the African controlled Food Chain, this should be the first economic activity that the African takes control of, we may not yet have access to our land, but the African is the market, the African must become the wholesaler and distributer, this will bring the land to the African, the land will return to the African, with the Food Chain.

Informal Trading:

The Non-African, hold the permits and licences to trade in all the white capitalist areas on South Africa, Alexandra residents, hundreds of small informal businesses, are not allowed to trade in Sandton, South Africa will become the Gateway to Africa's economy, if our African traders were allowed 'access' to the Non-African areas.

Very simply, I use Alexandra, because, if it was not for the 1913 Native Land Act, Sandton and Rosebank, would be Alexandra extensions 10 to 25, owned by the African population, and the white businesses now established in Sandton and Rosebank, accessed land that they had no accepted international constitutional right, through the restrictions placed on the African Community.

The African must not focus on 'claiming land' first priority is access to trade on the land illegally in the hands of the Non-African

Now to the land:

With regard to the land, the land was removed from the African people, all future consideration for land reform, should give priority to the subjugated, and those Blacks who have the financial ability to buy, assets to allow the Land Bank to finance them, should be excluded from Government support.

The rules of the game:

Our ancestors say, we must not follow the western concept of their game, and the rules and that protect the 'robbers'.

By introducing the 'Now Advantaged' grading class restrictions, we the Africanist, immediately remove the Colonization and Globalization, powerful mechanism to use the 'selected tribes', the selected political structures, the selected class, the selected caste, used to protect their wealth, and if the united Brotherhood of Man, unites around this Common Cause, we will change the rules of their game, and they will need to play according to our rules.

Those who talk about Land Expropriation without compensation, whether it is the EFF or the ANC, confirm that their political philosophy is entrenched in the protection of the western capitalist monopoly system, that subjugated the majority of our people, and that, except for the few, the rest of our population will remain subjugated, they give credit to the status that they believe is legal, they are taking the fight into the laws that protect the invader, and they know, the invader will be able to defend land expropriation, for the next 100 years.

Those who talk about Land Invasion, are admitting that they are going to invade the stolen land, protected by invaders laws, they encourage the 'still disadvantaged' to do invade land, for political expedience, and the invaders will punished accordingly, all in the name of political expedience.

The ancestors say, we must unite as Africanist Nationalists, we must identify the first people that bought the land in this country, the first owners of property, we must research the first property registrations, our research will identify the mining investors, who invested in agriculture land, and the message to those to bought our land illegally, according to our African custom;

"Our ancestors say that, we must unite with the common cause to have our land returned, and 'our land will return'"

As the Africanist believed in 1949, and Mr. BR Ambedkar's wise words in 1949, if we wish to become a nation, we need to become a *Brotherhood of Man*, a *fraternity*, and we will move to a Political / Social Democracy, let the people rule, let us give all, black and white, what we believe all people should enjoy, follow the Africanist of 1949, and let us start with the Africanist 'Bill of Rights'[15], ratified by the ANC in 1943, and the 1949 Programme of Action, let the Africanist reclaim their rightful place.

Our ancestors call for us to unite the Africanist in Africa with a common cause, the elders who were coerced into supporting the Charterists with empty promises, having to follow the 'love the white', will unite under the Brotherhood of Man. Those whites who wish to follow, will follow. As the wave moves through South Africa, and then Africa, the world will change.

Let us unite the people of Africa, as we unite in the Brotherhood of Man;

"OUR LAND WILL RETURN"

Cedric de la Harpe
"I am an African"

---

[15] *Copy available from author on request*

9 781718 699588